to Vidya Dehejia

from the Author

19. Jan. 2007.

You Hong june

Smiles of the Baby Buddha

Smiles of the Baby Buddha

Appreciating the cultural heritage of Kyŏngju

Yu Hong-june
Translated by Charles M. Mueller

Changbi Publishers, Inc.

Photo Credits
Kim Daebyuk   page 67, 68, 70
Ahn Jang-heon   page 33, 55, 76, 78, 97(left), 120(top), 186, 202(both), 217, 220, 241, 248, 263, 264
Kim Sŏngchŏl   page 14, 17, 27, 30, 43, 113, 125, 128, 153, 157, 213

First published by Changbi Publishers, Inc. 1999
Copyright © 1999 by Yu Hong-june

Smiles of the Baby Buddha
Appreciating the cultural heritage of Kyŏngju

by Yu Hong-june / translated by Charles M. Mueller

ISBN 89-364-7056-6 03810
Changbi Publishers, Inc.
513-11, Munbal-ri, Gyoha-eup, Paju-si,
Gyeonggi-do, 413-832, Korea
Tel. 82-31-955-3333
Fax. 82-31-955-3400
www.changbi.com
E-mail bildung@changbi.com

Printed and bound in the Republic of Korea

Contents

A Few Words to the Reader   7

INTRODUCTION   *Kyŏngju's History and Cultural Heritage*   11

PART 1   PULGUKSA TEMPLE
          There are No Flowers in Pulguksa Temple's Courtyard   47
          What did you Trust?   73

PART 2   STROLL THROUGH SŎRABŎL
          Smiles of the Baby Buddha   105
          Ah, Kamŭnsa Temple and Stupa!   130
          Emille Bell: Old Legends and New Facts   155

PART 3   Sŏkkuram
          Mt. Tohamsan's Sŏkpulsa Temple:
              A Glorious and Ignoble Past   183
          Pursuing the Mysteries of Sŏkkuram   211
          Even Inanimate Objects Have Life   240

Note   Charles M. Mueller   267

Map of Kyŏngju   269

A Few Words to the Reader

Any foreign visitor to Korea has probably heard of Kyŏngju's historical significance and its importance as a cultural site. For a millennium—beginning in the 1st century B.C.E. and ending in the 10th century C.E.——Kyŏngju, as the capital of the Shilla Dynasty, was where Korea's classical culture flourished. The historical relics scattered in and around Kyŏngju have turned the area into a virtual 'outdoor museum'. Realistically speaking, it is not possible for foreign visitors to go and see every one of these relics; indeed, more than a week is necessary merely to take in the major sights.

This book was designed to allow foreign visitors to have an authentic experience of Kyŏngju during a two or three-day itinerary. With this in mind, the book has been divided into two sections: Introduction as a guide for first-time visitors, and three parts as a collection of essays that provide deeper insights into the unique features of Korean and Kyŏngju culture.

The Introduction provides an outline of Kyŏngju's geographical location, history, and cultural relics. Instead of ordering my discussion around various artifacts, I have explained how Kyŏngju appeared during each period in Korean history. In a natural manner, I have described the circumstances under which each artifact was produced, along with its culturally unique features. By doing so, I hope to go beyond formal explanations of historical items, to make it easier for foreigners to gain an intimate sense of Korea's exotic history and culture.

In the three parts, I discuss the construction and intrinsic beauty of Kyŏngju's representative cultural artifacts such as Ch'ŏmsŏngdae, the Kamŭnsa Temple pagoda, Mt. Namsan's Buddha statues, The Emille Bell, Sŏkkuram, and Pulguksa Temple. I also provide frank discussion on how each relic has been preserved, and, in some cases, altered or even destroyed. In other words, in addition to describing the beauty of each relic, I have talked about its history——whether it be glorious or ignoble.

At this point, I feel it is necessary to provide some background knowledge for those reading the essays in three parts. In particular, I would like to talk about the ways in which Korean cultural relics, despite their greatness, have been destroyed or damaged.

If we look back through Korean history, we see that the country has undergone three wars in which the country was completely razed. The first occurred as Genghis Khan's armies invaded Korea's Koryŏ kingdom on seven occasions during the 13th century. At this time, all of the wooden buildings in Kyŏngju were burned to the ground. The gigantic Hwangnyongsa Temple was also leveled. The second destructive wave occurred at the end of the 16th century, when Japan's Toyotomi Hideyoshi launched two invasions during a seven-year period. At this time, Kyŏngju once more became a sea of fire, and numerous artifacts were stolen. The third occurred during the 1950 Korean War. Although Kyŏngju was not occupied by Communist forces, it was right up against the Naktong River front line. As a base for Korean and UN troops, it suffered tremendous damage. The fact that the UN headquarters was located at no other than Panwolsŏng (Half-Moon Fortress)——the site of the ancient Shilla palace——gives one a sense of the situation at the time.

While the above three periods of war caused tremendous damage,

Kyŏngju artifacts underwent the greatest damage during the 36 years of Japanese colonial rule during the first half of the 20th century. At this time, Japanese imperialists unearthed and plundered Kyŏngju's historical relics. Under the guise of 'excavation', countless tumuli were dug up. Even now, we are unable to find out just how many of the excavated articles were secretly spirited away. Countless Buddha statues and stone pagodas were also destroyed or stolen. Indeed, there doesn't seem to be a single historical relic that escaped damage.

In addition to such abuse at the hands of foreigners, Korean cultural relics were also scarred by Koreans' mistakes. Having won independence at the end of World War II, Korea was divided into North and South, and after the internecine fighting of the Korean War, South Korea fully set out on the course to modernization. With its sights set exclusively on economic development based on industrialization, Korea was able to move from agriculture to industry during the 1980s, transforming itself from an underdeveloped nation into a developing one. However in the quest for an exceedingly fast rate of progress in such a short period, much was sacrificed. For example, there was an almost blind adherence to Western values, which then were used to judge everything else. As a result, Koreans had virtually no pride or interest in discovering their own unique traditions. Moreover, Park Chung-hee, like other dictators before him, wielded the sword of tyranny before cultural relics. Due to him, Kyŏngju's artifacts received further scars as they were altered from their original state.

As an art historian, I've always regretted this situation. In an attempt to arouse Koreans' interest in their own culture, I wrote the first volume of the series *My Exploration of Cultural Heritage* published in 1993 in the form of a travelogue. Unexpectedly, there was an overwhelming reaction to that book, which became a million-seller. In my opinion, such positive response was brought about by Koreans' thirst for their own cultural identity. So far, three volumes have been published in the series. The sections in this book introducing Kyŏngju's historical relics were originally presented in those three volumes. In other words, this book was not written with the foreign reader in mind. Even so, this book has been published with the idea that it might serve as a guide to both the beauty and the faults of Kyŏngju, and by extension, an introduction to Korean culture.

Korea's Ministry of Culture and Tourism has provided the total costs of translating this book. I would like to express my deep gratitude to all those working under Minister Pak Chiwon, who has shown me much undeserved courtesy and exceptional determination, and to Shin Nakkyun, the former minister. And my gratitude to Charles M. Mueller, who undertook this translation, is beyond words. If this book serves as a good guidebook for foreigners visiting Kyŏngju, and if there are foreigners who come to understand Korean culture and the innate spirit of the people, I must give all credit to Charles.

The pictures in this book consist primarily of photos I've taken during more than 20 years of exploration. These have been augmented by the high-quality photos and illustrations of professional photographers such as Kim Daebyuk, Ahn Jang-heon and Kim Sŏngchŏl.

Along with readers, I would like to express my gratitude to these people for their kind help .

December 1999
Yu Hong-june

Introduction: Kyŏngju's History and Cultural Heritage

THE ANCIENT APPEARANCE OF KYŎNGJU AND THE BEAUTY OF ITS RUINS

Kyŏngju is a wide basin situated in the southeast corner of the Korean Peninsula. From Seoul, it is about 360 kilometers by car, 50 minutes by plane, and 4 hours by the Saemaŭl express train. Present-day Kyŏngju, which includes the peripheral areas formerly known as Wolsŏng County, measures 1,300 square kilometers and has a population of about 300,000, but the downtown area itself is around 200 square kilometers and has 150,000 residents. In Korea——a country with a high population density——it is only a small city.

However, during the millennium between the 1st century B.C.E. and the 10th century C.E., the city attained great affluence as the capital of the ancient Shilla kingdom. According to the 9th century records, it boasted a population of around 180 thousand, making it an East Asian metropolis on par with Chang-an, the capital of T'ang China. In other words, it was much larger than modern-day Kyŏngju.

Moreover, ancient records tell us that the city was laid out in a stately pattern of 1,360 blocks and that "the temples were numerous as the stars, and pagodas were like lines of geese." Its tallest building was

11

Hwangnyongsa Temple's nine-story pagoda, which stood in the very heart of the city. The body of this structure was 68 meters high, or 80 meters tall if the finial is included. We can get a sense of its imposing height when we consider that it was as tall as one of modern-day Kyŏngju's 20-floor high-rise apartments with a 15-meter aerial antenna on the roof. In the city's numerous tile-roofed houses, the use of oak charcoal to prevent excessive smoke during mealtime is yet another indication of the living standard of the period.

However, this pagoda, along with most other wooden structures, was lost to fire. At present, all that remains are relics impervious to fire, such as stone structures and sculptures. The remaining foundations of the ancient palace, government buildings, temples and houses, along with various stone fragments, mean that we can only imagine what the ancient city may have been like. On the other hand, the ancient Shilla tombs and the old building fragments rolling about the fields give the area a tranquil atmosphere, a certain charm that some people find fascinating. After all, even the popular Parthenon in Athens is but a 'ruin'.

KYŎNGJU DURING THE NEOLITHIC AND BRONZE AGES

In spite of its position in the southeast corner of the Korean Peninsula, Kyŏngju served as an ancient capital for a millennium——a feat made possible by its geopolitical features during the formation of Korea's ancient kingdoms.

As can be seen in the 'Timeline of Korean History' below, the nation's history, reaching back 500 thousand years to the Paleolithic Era, is as long as any people's. And, along with other civilizations, the roots of the Korean people began to form around 8,000 B.C.E. During Korea's Neolithic period, people lived near rivers or the sea in partially dug-out huts, making a living through both hunting and farming. Pottery has been found among the relics these people left behind. Because of its comb-like lines, it is commonly referred to as "comb-pattern pottery". For seven

Timeline of Korean History

500,000 Years Ago	Paleolithic Age
8,000 B. C. E.——1,000 B. C. E.	Neolithic Age
1,000 B. C. E.——100 B. C. E.	Bronze Age
100 B. C. E.——668 C. E.	Three Kingdoms period
	(Koguryŏ, Paekche, Shilla)
668 C. E.——935 C. E.	Unified Shilla
918 C. E.——1392 C. E.	Koryŏ
1392 C. E.——1910 C. E.	Chosŏn
1910 C. E.——1945 C. E.	Japanese Occupation

long, tedious millennia leading up to the Neolithic Period, during which the culture of the comb-pattern pottery people continued unchanged, Kyŏngju did not appear on the stage of Korean history.

Around 1000 B. C. E., the society on the Korean Peninsula underwent a tremendous change. Part of the Tungus people living in Mongolia migrated to the Korean Peninsula, conquering and assimilating the comb-pattern pottery people. In doing so, they created a new society and a true agricultural culture. They were skilled in the use of bronze and used 'patternless pottery' instead of the comb-pattern pottery. For this reason, archaeologists refer to this people as the Bronze Age 'patternless pottery people'.

Historically, this period is that of Ancient Chosŏn (not to be confused with the later Chosŏn Dynasty) and the Three Han. At this time, Kyŏngju was controlled by several sanguineous clans belonging to the China— one of the three tribal confederations. These clans, known as the 'Six Villages of Saro', represented Kyŏngju's debut on the stage of Korean history.

STONE INSCRIPTION AT CH'ŎNJŎN-RI This drawing, inscribed by Bronze-age people during the third century B.C.E., shows that they regarded this area as sacred. The meaning of these mysterious geometrical designs is still not known.

Unlike most areas in Korea, Kyŏngju boasted a wide prairie that was ideal for Bronze Age farmers, mountains rising on all four sides of the basin provided natural protection from enemies. The above-mentioned name 'Saro' and Kyŏngju's ancient name 'Sŏrabŏl' both come from the phrase '*so-ŭi pŏlp'an*' (cow's prairie). Countless cattle leisurely munching on grass across the wide prairie must have been a striking sight. Even now, Kyŏngju's Sannaemyŏn area is famous for its roast beef.

The area's Bronze Age lasted until the 1st century B.C.E. Traces of Kyŏngju's Bronze Age residents can be seen in the dolmen (a representative symbolic relic of the Bronze Age in Korea) and in picture inscriptions on rock faces. Many dolmen can be seen scattered in the vicinity of Kŏnch'ŏn on the western outskirts of Kyŏngju. The rock pictures found only in the Kyŏngju area indicate that the group of people who moved into the area around this time was from Siberia. The rock inscription pictures found to the south of Kyŏngju at Pan'gudae and Ch'ŏnjŏn Village in Ulsan's Ŏnyangmyŏn, along with those found to the northeast of Kyŏngju at Ch'ilp'o in P'ohang, are representative relics from the period. Although these pictures show realistic images of animals, they are also covered with abstract, geometric patterns that have an air of beauty and mystery. By car, they are all within an hour from Kyŏngju.

Thus, Kyŏngju's Saro villages slowly emerged during the Bronze Age, fully to appear on the stage of history around the 1st century B.C.E. as the Bronze Age ended. At this time, as iron culture spread throughout the Korean Peninsula, ancient states emerged from the tribal confederacies. As a part of this shift, the Saro villages finally developed into the Saro state—the predecessor of Shilla.

FORMATION OF THE ANCIENT STATES (1ST CENTURY B.C.E. TO 4TH CENTURY C.E.) AND SHILLA TOMBS

According to the record *Samguk Sagi* (*Historical Records of the Three Kingdoms*), Saro was founded in 57 B.C.E. This is merely the date when Saro's new ruling class took power: the entity was still not a full-fledged monarchy.

During this period, tribal groups throughout Korea and Manchuria were making the transition to ancient monarchical states. In the 5th century, this process finally spawned the kingdoms of Koguryŏ, Paekche, and Shilla. For this reason, Korea's ancient historical period is often referred to as the Three Kingdoms period, and even the era prior to the formation of these states is sometimes called the Proto-Three Kingdoms period.

If we look at Shilla politics during this latter period, we find, in addition to the 'Six Villages', three clans (Pak, Sŏk, and Kim) that rose to prominence and eventually overcame the six villages to form the ruling class.

These three clans each wielded significant political and economic clout based on their respective power bases: members of the Pak clan served as ritual officiators, a kind of shamanic leader; those of the Sŏk clan were responsible for iron production; and those of the Kim clan, gold production. If we were to imagine Kyŏngju as an egg, these three clans could be said to have controlled its yolk. The Pak clan had controlled

Kyŏngju's Orŭng (Five Tombs) area and Kŭmsŏng, where Najŏng was located. The Sŏk clan was in Wolsŏng, and the Kim clan was in the Kyerim area.

In the 4th century during the reign of King Naemul, Shilla finally developed a monarchical system. Around this time, Shilla went from a confederation of clans in which the three clans took turns providing a leader to one in which the Kim clan held total power. From this time, the title of king (*maripkan*) came into use along with linear succession of the crown within the Kim clan; in other words, Shilla was, from this point on, a true monarchy.

From the onset of the Kim royal line in the 4th century, Shilla began constructing massive tombs in order to emphasize the authority of the Shilla king and nobles. The tombs that now stand as high as small hills in the middle of Kyŏngju were built continuously from this period up until Shilla's demise in the 10th century. From what would have then been just north of Wolsŏng, the Shilla fortress, groups of tombs can be seen here and there to the west, in the general vicinity of the Taerŭng'won (Great Tumuli Park) area, Orŭng area, Nodong-dong, Nosŏ-dong, and Sŏak-dong area. Currently, there are 155 confirmed Shilla tombs. Since there were only 56 Shilla kings, two-thirds of these tombs must belong to noblemen such as General Kim Yu-shin.

With the eventual expansion of Kyŏngju's urban area in the modern age, houses have been built throughout the tomb areas. As visitors look at the residences standing between the ancient tombs, they truly get the sense that they are in a millennium-old city. In this respect, these tombs are both the outer face of Kyŏngju and its greatest symbol.

All of these tombs were built on a grand scale. Ponghwangdae, the biggest, is 22 meters high. Its circumference at its base measures 250 meters. The most famous of these, Ch'ŏnmach'ong (Heavenly Horse Tomb) at Taerŭng'won, is 16 meters high and 157 meters around the base. Among the tombs, those from the 5th and 6th centuries are

In Kyongju, around 155 large tumuli such as this remain. Indeed, the image of Kyongju that leaves visitors with the strongest impression is the royal tombs giant size and soft curvature.

particularly large. Some of the tombs are in pairs (with one slightly larger), allowing for the burial of married couples.

Any visitor to Kyŏngju wandering around Taerŭng'won or Orŭng can feel a warm breeze from the distant past when admiring these 1500-year-old tumuli. Taerŭng'won and Orŭng are only open during the day, but one can visit those in Nodong-dong and Nosŏ-dong at night to enjoy a charm and romance only to be found in Kyŏngju. In particular, this area is home to Kŭmgwanch'ong, where a golden crown (*kŭmgwan*) was discovered, as well as to Sŏbongch'ong. The latter was named by the Swedish Prince Gustav, who participated in its excavation. As for the tumuli discovered during the early 20th century, many of the mounds had disappeared, leaving a barren circle. Now that they've been planted

In Kyongju, five gold crowns from the Shilla period have been unearthed. These reconfirm that Shilla was the royal nation of gold. Bearing designs depicting sacred trees and antlers, these crowns have been further decorated with mysterious curved pieces of jade.

with grass, they are nice places for quiet rests.

When one looks at the curves of Kyŏngju's tumuli reaching up toward the heavens, one imagines sets of beautiful waves crossing the earth. With their graceful curvature, they almost seem to be moving towards the viewer. They also have an erotic atmosphere, like the outline of a lover's breasts or hip — an impression that is particularly strong when they are seen at night. Of course, as the Shilla tumuli changed during each era, there were minor changes in the form of tombs. In addition, carved stones were eventually added as decoration.

Kyŏngju tumuli were situated in sites close enough to be viewed from the palace. This fact, along with their complex and massive internal structures, was enough to deter most grave robbers. In tombs created around the late 4th century onward, excavations have unearthed a large number of pure-gold burial objects such as gold crowns, earrings, bracelets and jade necklaces, as well as several thousand pieces of pottery.

At present, five gold crowns from Shilla have been discovered. The gold used in decorative items found in Ch'ŏnmach'ong alone comes to around 3 kilograms! Most of these artifacts are now on display at either the National Museum of Korea or the National Museum of Kyŏngju. If one takes a trip to Taerŭng'won, one can get a sense of the number of relics excavated from these tombs. For this reason, Kyŏngju may be called 'the royal capital of tombs', and Shilla 'the kingdom of gold'. Indeed, it is no accident that one out of every eight Koreans has the surname Kim, which means 'gold'.

EXPANSION OF SHILLA ROYAL AUTHORITY (5TH TO 7TH CENTURY C.E.) AND BUDDHIST CULTURE

Following the establishment of the Kim clan monarchy during the reign of King Naemul in the 4th century, Shilla spent the 5th and 6th centuries taking on the trappings of an ancient state. Historians often mention three characteristics common to all ancient states: first, a strong monarchy and a system of rules and regulations; second, territorial expansion and an increase in production; and third, the creation of a guiding ideology based on religion. Shilla too acquired these three elements around this time.

During the reign of Shilla's King Chijŭng (r. 500-514), the advanced political system of the Chinese acted as a stimulus. As a part of its new system, Shilla changed its name from Saro to Shilla and changed the title of the king from the pure-Korean 'maripkan' to the Chinese-derived 'wang'. From this point, the nation actually took on the name 'Shilla kingdom'. Soon after, King Pŏphŭng (r. 514-540) proclaimed edicts making Shilla a nation centrally controlled by the aristocracy. These changes represent the first characteristic of ancient states mentioned above.

Shilla's economy made rapid progress. In the 5th century, a large market is said to have opened in Kyŏngju, selling items from all over; and in the 6th century, during King Chijŭng's reign, farmers began to use cattle for plowing. Numerous irrigation facilities were also established, as the kingdom steadily increased its productive capacity.

In modern terms, Shilla achieved rapid economic growth and an increase in its GNP. During this period, King Chijŭng conquered Ullŭng Island (Usan'guk) and King Pŏphŭng annexed Central Kaya, expanding Shilla territory to the Naktong River.

In addition to Shilla, the other ancient states of Koguryŏ and Paekche were also making efforts to expand their territories. Koguryŏ, situated to the north, was the strongest of the three states and the first to develop culturally. As it began to exert pressure on Shilla and Paekche, these two states entered into an alliance in order to resist Koguryŏ's advance. Shilla's King Chinhŭng (540-576), along with Paekche's King Sŏng'wang, launched an attack against Koguryŏ that succeeded in recovering land in the Han River basin. But then King Chinhŭng, in a somewhat unscrupulous move, arbitrarily broke the alliance and made a surprise attack on Paekche, obliterating the Paekche forces and taking sole possession of the Han River basin. It thus became a major power occupying the area as far north as Wonsan and Hamhŭng.

In this fashion, Shilla, which had been the weakest of the three kingdoms and had been the last to develop culturally, rose to be the new power on the Korean Peninsula. In particular, expansion into the Han River basin enabled it to have direct commerce with China. Shilla had therefore fulfilled the second requisite of an ancient state.

Third, Shilla imported the ideology known as Buddhism. Its indigenous faith had been shamanism. The symbolic trees and deer antlers on the

Shilla crowns, the legend of Shilla's founders being born from eggs, and the excavation of 24 bull horns from Ch'ŏnmach'ong all point to the kingdom's shamanic past. However, as Shilla developed into an ancient state, a feeble ideology such as shamanism was inadequate for maintaining the state. A more sophisticated belief system that could provide the people with a common philosophy was badly needed. Shilla, like all other East Asian states, solved this problem through the acceptance of Buddhism.

Shilla received Buddhism in the 5th century, making it the last of the Three Kingdoms to do so. Its formal acceptance of Buddhism, however, had to wait another hundred years, until the 6th century. This late introduction of Buddhism was due to opposition from adherents to indigenous beliefs.

After all, one aspect of the introduction of Buddhism was a strengthening of monarchical and aristocratic authority. In a sense, the Buddha and bodhisattvas in Buddhism corresponded to the king and nobles in the social realm. It logically followed that, as believers had faith in the Buddha, the people had to be obedient to the king. Both ideology and faith thus fit together like two parts of a puzzle. For this reason, indigenous forces opposed the introduction of Buddhism. Even so, the king and nobles actively promoted the new faith so that, in 535, during the reign of King Pŏphŭng, it was finally accepted through the martyrdom of Yi Ch'adon, a minister close to the king. After this time, Shilla's Buddhist culture developed by leaps and bounds.

Shilla melded Buddhism with its national ideology to form 'National Protection Buddhism' based on the idea that "the King is identical to the Buddha." Buddhist ethical rules were associated with military organization to found an aristocratic youth corps of officers known as the Hwarang, which would serve to symbolize the Shilla military. The frequent occurrence of the word 'hwarang' in the names of modern organizations or places related to the military, as seen in the use of

'Hwarangdae' for the Military Academy of Korea, stems from this ancient youth corps.

Moreover, great monks such as Wonhyo and Ŭisang appeared, further advancing Buddhism in Korea. Wonhyo advocated a Buddhism for the masses, giving hope to the common people, while Ŭisang used logical exposition to provide the king and aristocracy with a refined ruling ideology. Eventually, this formed the consciousness that enabled Shilla, the weakest of the Three Kingdoms, to emerge as the final victor.

BUDDHIST ARTIFACTS OF THE SHILLA DYNASTY

After the official recognition of Buddhism, Kyŏngju witnessed the erection of numerous Buddhist monasteries and statues. The fact that in Kuhwang-dong (Nine Emperor Ward), there were Hwangnyongsa Temple, Hwangboksa Temple, Punhwangsa Temple, and six other monasteries with the character 'hwang' ('emperor') in their names is just one indication of Buddhism's rapid growth in the kingdom. Of these monasteries, Hwangnyongsa Temple was the most symbolic. The construction of this monastery, which came to 9,000 *p'yŏng* (30 acres) in total area, began in 553. It is said that the wall took 17 years to build. Its nine-story wooden pagoda stood around 80 meters high. The structure was burned down during the 13th-century Mongol invasions, but the foundation stones still remain for visitors to see. If one has visited old temples in Kyoto or Nara in Japan, it may be pointed out that the pagodas at Kyoto's Kofukuji or the five-story pagoda at Nara's Horyuji are actually built in styles imported from Korea during the Three Kingdoms period and that the Hwangnyongsa Temple pagoda stood two times higher and covered an area four times larger than the latter. Next to the empty site of Hwangnyongsa Temple, there is the small Punhwangsa Temple. A peculiar feature of this temple is its pagoda, which was built using stones shaped like bricks. Only three stories now remain, but, originally, this too was nine stories high. In constructing this pagoda, the

RECREATED MODEL OF HWANGNYONGSA TEMPLE
Although it is no longer extant, a recreated model of Hwangnyongsa Temple shows the imposing majesty of its precise proportions and grand scale.

builders utilized stone on the model of Chinese brick pagodas, which in turn were an innovation from wooden pagodas. After unification, the stone pagoda became the main type of Shilla pagodas.

According to records, Hwangnyongsa Temple and Punhwangsa Temple had bronze Buddha statues measuring 4.8 meters high, but these were destroyed in temple fires. Unfortunately, the only extant Shilla Buddhist statues from the pre-unification period are the small gilt-bronze Buddha and stone Buddha now on display at Museum. The figures in the stone statues known as the Samhwaryŏng Baby Buddhas, delight visitors to Kyŏngju National Museum with their innocent and childlike expressions. These figures were originally situated on Mt. Namsan, a mountain considered sacred during the Unified Shilla period. Prior to unification, there were already four places on Mt. Namsan that had carvings of Buddha figures.

The Samhwaryŏng Baby Buddhas have since been moved into the museum, but on the base of nearby Mt. Namsan, one still finds the T'apkok Buddha in relief and a 7th-century Shilla figure known as the

Niche (Kamshil) Buddha, both carved onto rock faces. Of these two pieces, the Niche Buddha has a deeply compassionate countenance resembling a Shilla (Korean) person— an indication that Shilla Buddhism sought truth in everyday reality rather than in an absolute deity. This perspective corresponds well to Wonhyo's ideal of a Buddhism of and for the people.

There was, of course, a gigantic palace in the Shilla kingdom. No longer able to witness its grandeur, we must content ourselves with a look at its foundation. From the time of the Saro kingdom, Shilla's royal palace was situated at Panwolsŏng, next to which the National Museum of Kyŏngju now stands. However, we cannot surmise what Panwolsŏng originally looked like. We only know that, instead of being circular, it was shaped like a half-moon, with the idea that the full moon gradually wanes whereas the half-moon gets bigger.

Moreover, the grand government buildings that stood at the site have all burned down, leaving only their foundation stones. Only the symbolic Ch'ŏmsŏngdae remains intact in the spot where the astronomical observatory stood. This stone observatory, bottle-shaped and standing 10 meters high, is known as the oldest observatory in Asia. However, this structure, rather than serving as a building for the actual observation of stellar constellations, possessed a wonderful symbolism that has become famous. With 360 stones, 30 layers, and a central window with 12 layers above and below, the structure symbolizes the year (by lunar calendar), with 12 months and 360 days. This sort of symbolism often found its way into Shilla architecture. After unification, Shilla's cultural genius underwent considerable development, enabling it to achieve perfect classical beauty in sculptures and architecture such as those at Sŏkkuram and Pulguksa Temple.

THE UNIFIED SHILLA PERIOD (668-935) AND THE PERFECTION OF CLASSICAL BEAUTY

Amidst the frequent wars and tensions that characterized the East Asian political situation during the 7th century, nations were moving towards the formation of unified states. At the end of the 6th century (589), China, which had been split between Northern and Southern Dynasties, was unified under Sui but gave way to the T'ang Dynasty (612) after two failed attacks on Koguryŏ.

Unable to form an ancient state, Japan had been ruled by clan alliances, but in the early 7th century, Prince Shotoku appeared on the scene, strengthening central authority. In 645, he unified Japan under the imperial system.

On the Korean Peninsula, Koguryŏ, Paekche, and Shilla continued the struggle to expand their respective territories. Koguryŏ, the strongest of these, fought two life-or-death wars with Sui, followed by an extensive war with T'ang. While victorious, much of Koguryŏ's strength was expended in these wars, a situation made worse by internal revolts. Paekche was in a groggy state, reeling from Shilla's surprise attack in the Han River basin. As Koguryŏ and Paekche seemed poised to form a coalition to attack Shilla, the latter, as Korea's new power, formed an alliance with T'ang China and launched preemptory attack on Paekche, destroying it in 660 before conquering Koguryŏ in 668. Shilla thus succeeded in unifying the Three Kingdoms.

However, the T'ang recruits who had volunteered on Shilla's behalf in the war for unification remained, intent on seizing the Korean Peninsula. As a result, Shilla fought a ten-year war with T'ang China, successfully driving out the remaining soldiers in 676. In this way, Shilla achieved victory in the war for unification, but its power only extended from the Taedong River to the 39th parallel at Wonsan Bay. Manchuria to the north was held by Palhae, a state created by Koguryŏ refugees and the Malgal tribe. This incomplete unification signified the limits of Shilla's military and cultural capacity, and in the end, meant that Korean territory thereafter would be restricted to the peninsula.

Nevertheless, the Shilla unification was significant as a union of peoples living on the Korean Peninsula. If it had been unable to achieve unification, the peninsula would have probably fallen prey to Balkanization. Moreover, Shilla actively introduced Paekche and Koguryŏ culture. Thus the ideal of ancient state, as envisioned by the Three Kingdoms, finally achieved its realization with Shilla's classical beauty.

Unified Shilla culture reached its zenith a hundred years after unification, in the mid-8th century during the reign of King Kyŏngdŏk (r. 742-765). The most epresentative historical artifacts that remain in Kyŏngju today, i.e. Sŏkkuram, Pulguksa Temple, Sŏkka Pagoda, Tabo Pagoda, Emille Bell, and Buddhist statues on Mt. Namsan, were all either created or completed at this time.

UNIFIED SHILLA ARCHITECTURE

Perhaps the most spectacular relics from this period were the wooden buildings such as those in the royal palace, but these have all been destroyed by either war or the passage of time, leaving only those structures built out of a hard, durable material— i.e., granite. Thus, the artifacts to be introduced here are almost all made of stone. It is at least heartening to think that pagodas, one of the most representative Shilla artifacts, have survived.

Pagodas (or stupas) in India originally took the form of earthen tombs, but in China, they were created in the form of wooden structures. These then were introduced into the Three Kingdoms as the main pagoda style and also transmitted to Japan via Paekche and Koguryŏ. However, China eventually developed the brick pagoda as the form appropriate to its culture, whereas Korea developed stone pagodas using stacked blocks of granite. Japan, on the other hand, continued to make pagodas using wood. This is because China had plenty of clay with which to make bricks as well as expertise using kilns, while Korea had copious amounts of hard granite and Japan plenty of timber. As a result, the three nations of East Asia each developed their own unique style of pagoda.

KAMŬNSA TEMPLE PAGODA   Although the temple no longer exists, the majestic pair of three-story pagodas that has survived provides a glimpse into the spirit of the Shilla people of this period.

Korean stone pagodas began in the early 7th century in Paekche. A style of stone pagoda was created, beginning with the nine-story stone pagoda at Mirŭksa Temple in Iksan, which eventually developed into the five-story pagoda at Chŏngnimsa Temple. However, Paekche fell at this point and its pagoda construction techniques were thus transmitted to Unified Shilla, where they eventually led to the typical style of the three-story stone pagoda.

The initial style of the Unified Shilla three-story pagoda can be seen in the Kamŭnsa Temple pagoda. Built in commemoration of King Munmu's illustrious deeds, Kamŭnsa Temple was situated close to Taewang'am (king rock)——the place where the cremated king's ashes had been placed in the sea. Kamŭnsa Temple's three-story pagoda, in the tradition of the pagoda at Paekche's Chŏngnimsa Temple, had a cheerful sense of transcendence. At the same time, it had a sense of firm stability not to be found in the Chŏngnimsa pagoda.

If one looks at the overall proportions of the Kamŭnsa Temple pagoda, one can trace a straight line running at an 80-degree angle from the corners of the base, through the corners of the eaves on the three roof stones, to the top of the finial. If one then looks at the height of the stone blocks making up the body of the pagoda, the first one is refreshingly tall, while the second and third gradually taper off. The height of the first story's body is equal to the length of one side of the lower base, so that an equilateral triangle coming up from the lower base would reach to the top of the first story's body. Moreover, the width of the body stones of each story from bottom to top are set in a proportion of 4:3:2.

Through such a sense of geometric proportion, the Kamŭnsa Temple pagoda was able to simultaneously provide a sense of stability and transcendence——two aesthetic qualities that are normally antithetical. This pagoda's impact becomes evident when we consider the following facts: 90% of Unified Shilla pagodas were stone pagodas; 90% of these were three-story pagodas; and these three-story pagodas basically followed the proportions of the Kamŭnsa pagoda. In the end, the Kamŭnsa Temple pagoda gave birth to an outstanding stylistic form, so pervasive that Korea was often referred to as 'the land of the stone pagoda'. The nearly perfect refinement of the three-story pagoda was to be seen approximately a century later, with the completion of Sŏkka Pagoda in Pulguksa Temple.

Today, nothing remains of Unified Shilla's temple architecture. However, the solemn temple layout and the beautiful and firm stone embankments of Pulguksa Temple still remain as a reminder of this period. For this reason, in 1970 the temple was reconstructed in its present form. At Pulguksa Temple, buildings were spaced evenly, having been positioned according to geometric proportions based on the equilateral triangle, the circle, the cross-secting line of a square (2 squared), etc. The stone embankments, on the other hand, combined natural and carved stone in a number of ways so as to form a splendid

AN OVERHEAD VIEW OF
PULGUKSA (BUDDHA LAND)
TEMPLE
*The temple's central area,
consisting of twin
pagodas along with the
Buddha Hall, expresses
the solemn atmosphere of
the Hwaŏm Pure Land.
When founded, it also
served as a symbol of the
kingdom's power and
authority.*

harmony between the man-made and the natural. The embankment in front of the temple basically consists of carved stones stacked atop natural stones. And the upper section is formed by placing natural stones within a frame of carved stones. This very harmonious and natural movement from the natural to the man-made also emphasizes the fantastic crafted beauty of the embankment under the belfry of Pŏmyŏngnu (Floating Reflection Pavilion).

In the courtyard in front of Pulguksa Temple's Main Buddha Hall, there is a pair of pagodas: the three-story Sŏkka Pagoda and Tabo Pagoda. The latter has been constructed in the pavilion style. The extremely simple Sŏkka Pagoda contrasts with the complex structure of Tabo Pagoda. Whereas the former is elegant, the latter is highly ornate. Perhaps Kim Pushik summed this up best in his 12th-century work *Samguk Sagi*,

TABO PAGODA
Modeled on tall pavilions, the exquisite
structure of the Tabo Pagoda is the
acme of ornate elegance. Even so, the
structure strikes one as noble and not
extravagant in the least.

where he described Sŏkka Pagoda as "simple yet not squalid" and Tabo Pagoda as "ornate yet not extravagant". These words could also be used to describe Korea's unique aesthetic, whether it be that of Unified Shilla or that of the Chosŏn period.

This distinctive aesthetic can also be seen in the architectural works of Unified Shilla such as Anapchi (Goose and Duck Pond). Situated across from Panwolsŏng, Anapchi was an annex to the ancient Shilla palace. On this spot, an artificial pond was built as a part of a garden. The stone embankments have made it possible to restore the site to its present condition. As with the pagodas mentioned above, the basic concept underlying this structure is harmony between artificial and natural elements. The halls that stood at the site were made up of straight and diagonal lines, whereas the garden employed natural curves. These straight lines and curves provided a very appropriate sense of rugged

ANAPCHI This beautiful man-made lake achieves an exquisite harmony between the natural and man-made. With sharp curves along its edge and three islands in the middle, the lakes over-all scale cannot be taken in all at once from any vantage point.

irregularity that broke up the monotony and, at the same time, provided a sense of striking change.

Three islands were built within the pond so that the bank, in its entirety, is not visible from any vantage point. Indeed, the only way to see the entire pond at a glance is through an aerial photo. For this reason, Anapchi, in spite of its small size, looks like a giant lake and provides a diverse range of pleasures. Taking a stroll around the lake, you sometimes feel as if you were in the corner of a valley, and then as if you were in a forest or by a vast lake. And, at other times, you find yourself looking at a pavilion next to the shore. Such a pond, which expresses so well the harmony between the natural and the man-made, cannot be found in any other country or era. It is a unique heritage of Anapchi and the Unified Shilla period.

UNIFIED SHILLA SCULPTURE

Besides the gilt-bronze Buddha statues on display at the museum, Unified Shilla sculptures include the splendid Buddhist carvings at Sŏkkuram and on Mt. Namsan. Sŏkkuram is a man-made grotto situated on a slope near the summit of Mt. T'ohamsan. It commands an extensive view of the East Sea (Sea of Japan). Unlike other stone grottoes such as those in India's Ajanta or at China's Tunhuang or Yungang, which were created by cutting a cave out of stone, Sŏkkuram was made by carving thousands of stones which were then fit together to form a round dome. The grotto's dynamic structure and technology verge on the miraculous.

Sŏkkuram's master plan also consists of perfect geometrical proportions. Even in the actual implementation of this plan, the cave has no more than one-millimeter error per 10 meters. In other words, it has an inaccuracy rate of less than 1/10,000. Such technological know-how, which allowed workmen living 1,300 years ago to carve hard granite so accurately, is truly amazing.

Inside this solemn structure, the Sŏkkuram carvings are situated

BÙDDHA IN SÒKKURAM *The solemn appearance of the absolute as imagined by the people of the Unified Shilla Dynasty was expressed through this Buddha statue. This was also the ideal image of man.*

according to a definite iconography (in Buddhism, a "mandala"), which we still do not fully understand. Within the grotto, there are carvings of a total of 40 Buddhist figures, i.e., the Buddha, Bodhisattvas, Heavenly Kings, Devas, and the Ten Disciples. These sculptures one and all possess a classical beauty depicting the ideal of humanity. Buddha statue signifies the encounter between the divine and the human. In other words, it is the humanization of God and the deification of man. Such a depiction expresses both dignity and compassion. When both of these aspects are present, we call such artwork 'the harmonious ideal of beauty'. For this reason, Sŏkkuram's Buddha is the representation of the absolute that has had the deepest impact on the Korean consciousness. It is thus little surprise that the early morning excursion to Sŏkkuram has become the most basic tour course for visitors to Kyŏngju.

However, when visitors actually arrive at Sŏkkuram, they are often disappointed. There is a glass pane, set up to preserve the grotto, that prevents visitors from approaching the figures. And throngs of tourists make it even more difficult to properly appreciate the site. For such disheartened souls, I would like to recommend the Buddha statues on Mt. Namsan.

Kyŏngju's Mt. Namsan is a long mountain rising up sharply from behind the old palace site of Wolsŏng and the museum, to the south of Kyŏngju's downtown area. Since Korea has a plethora of Namsans (literally, "South Mountain"), one should always refer to it specifically as "Mt. Namsan in Kyŏngju". With the two peaks of Kŭmobong (468 meters) and Kowibong (494 meters), this large, oval-shaped mountain stretches 8 kilometers from north to south and 4 kilometers from west to east. Since the entire mountain is made up of granite rocks, on clear days, the sun's rays shimmer and sparkle as they glance off the rock faces. The lower slopes and base of the mountain are covered with dirt, but even this is actually broken granite boulders overlaid with soil. For this reason, only strong pines, oaks, bamboo, chrysanthemums, maples, and other native

THREE-STORY PAGODA AT THE YONGJANGSA TEMPLE SITE IN MT. NAMSAN There are about 200 Buddhist relics, including pagodas, Buddha statues and rock carved Buddhas, in Kyongju's Mt. Namsan. On the mountains slope looking out over a wonderful view, the Yongjangsa Temple site is one of the highlights of a field-trip to Mt. Namsan in Kyongju. Besides this three-story pagoda, there is a Buddhist carving sitting atop a high pedestal as well as a relief carved in fine detail.

Korean trees with strong vitality can grow here. This is just one more reason why this mountain is so dear to Koreans.

On Kyŏngju's Mt. Namsan, there are over 40 large and small valleys. The trails leading up each valley take one past pagodas, foundation stones of old temples and Buddha statues carved by the ancient Shilla people. From around 600 C.E. (the period preceding unification), sculptors began to carve Buddha statues on this mountain. By the Unified Shilla period, Mt. Namsan was considered to be a sacred realm where the Buddha resided. Reminders of the Buddha appeared throughout the area as artists worked to recreate the Buddhist Pure Land (paradise) here on earth. These "traces" of the Buddha numbered around 200, of which over 40 still remain. As a result, this mountain could be called a giant, open-air museum.

The most representative valleys are the Puch'ŏ, T'ap, Chŏl, Yaksu, Yongjang, and Samnŭng Valleys, while the most representative Buddha statues are those at Ch'ilbul-ram Hermitage, the Yongjangsa Temple site, the Sangsa-am rock-carved Buddha, the Yaksukol stone Buddha, Paeri village Buddha Triad, and the stone Buddha at Porisa Temple in Puch'ŏkol. I believe that the Shilla people's enshrinement of so many Buddhist statues on Kyŏngju's Mt. Namsan stems from the indigenous worship of mountains combined with messianic Buddhist thought.

In general, these statues were carved between the 7th and 9th centuries. As a result, they tend to be in an idealistic style. However, since they were carved onto rock faces, they have an abstract rather than a realistic appearance. Yet the beauty of the Mt. Namsan figures lies in their mysterious harmony with unadorned nature. Once again, this is the harmonious and idealistic aesthetic witnessed in Unified Shilla's architecture——a reflection of the harmony between the natural and the man-made.

With the advent of the Chosŏn Dynasty in the 14th century, the nation's leading ideology switched from Buddhism to Confucianism. As a result, the Buddha statues on Kyŏngju's Mt. Namsan entered a period of crisis. Due to severe persecution and a movement to destroy Buddhist icons, almost all of the Buddhist statues suffered heavy damage. Much of what remained was then plundered during the Japanese occupation. It saddens one to think that the Buddhist figures that remain often have broken-off heads and noses or are buried in dirt.

In spite of this, Mt. Namsan still has a remarkable ability to endure. To better preserve the relics, tourist development on Mt. Namsan has not been allowed. Even so, it is a fantastic course for visitors who truly want

Paeri Village Buddha Triad *Situated on the lower slopes of Mt. Namsan, this Buddha triads archaic smile is extremely enchanting. Childlike Buddha figures with such smiles are a style generally thought to date from the early 7th century.*

to understand and enjoy Kyŏngju. A guide is necessary to enjoy this area. Otherwise, it is easy to get lost and impossible to find the Buddhist carvings, which seem to hide and conceal themselves in the brush better than the Vietcong during the Vietnamese War.

It takes four or five days to thoroughly enjoy Kyŏngju. On the other hand, if you are one those foreign visitors who can hike (all Koreans are good hikers), you can pack a lunch and hike from morning to evening. It is thus possible to enjoy one-third of Mt. Namsan's Buddhist carvings in a single day. This, Mt. Namsan's main course, goes past Samnŭngkol, Sangsa-am, a rock carving of Buddha, the Mt. Kŭmosan summit, Yongjangsa Temple's pagoda and another Buddha in relief, Shinsŏn-am,

Porisa Temple's Seated Stone Buddha
Situated in Puchŏgol Valley on the slope of Kyŏngju's
Mt. Namsan, the Porisa Buddha Statue was carved during
the late 8th century. Many people adore this figure's
splendid visage and magnanimous smile.
With a human beauty more prominent than
that of the Sŏkkuram Buddha, this figure still sits in the open
air where visitors can appreciate it freely.

Ch'ilbul-ram, and the twin pagodas in Namsan-dong.

For those who are unable to hike, I would recommend a stroll along the northeastern flank of Mt. Namsan—a course that goes by the Medicine Buddha at Porisa Temple, the rock carving of Buddha in T'apkok, and the Niche Buddha. Porisa Temple's Medicine Buddha is an idealistic sculpture that looks like a miniature version of the Sŏkkuram Buddha. With its beautiful face and body and exceedingly charming smile, it has been dubbed "Mr. Unified Shilla".

The T'apkok (Pagoda Valley) rock carving of Buddha and the Pulgok (Buddha Valley) Niche Buddha are Shilla carvings predating unification. As such, they are the most characteristic of Shilla carvings, full of mystery and human beauty. This course should be taken by chartering a taxi. If one wants to save expenses, it is possible to take a taxi to Porisa Temple and then see T'apkok and the Niche Buddha, from which the museum comes into view. One can then go to the museum by following the stream and then the road. If one tries to walk this route in the opposite direction, however, the lack of signs or guide posts will make it impossible to find a road at the end. By taxi, the route takes 2 hours, or, at a more leisurely pace, 3 hours.

In the museum hangs the Emille Bell, another artifact that amply demonstrates the outstanding craftsmanship of the Unified Shilla period. Weighing 20 tons, measuring 3.8 meters high and 7 meters thick, this giant bell is the largest in the world. It is famous for its lovely tone—a long, resonating echo that is said to sound like the word "emille" ("mother"). The Buddhist fairies and designs on the surface of the bell amply testify to the dreams and aesthetic vision of the Unified Shilla people. It is no longer struck, but at regular intervals, the museum plays a recording.

Korean Beauty After the Unified Shilla Period: Mountain Temples and *Yangban* Architecture

Unified Shilla fell to Koryŏ in 935; yet Kyŏngju's glory had already ebbed by the 9th century. From this point on, the culture limped along worn paths. But the decline of Unified Shilla culture, which centered on Kyŏngju, did not signify the degeneration of Korean culture as a whole. On the contrary, this period set the stage for a new development——the aristocratic culture of Korea's Middle Ages.

By the 9th century, the social structure of the Unified Shilla kingdom was already undergoing significant changes: i.e., the gradual devolution of power from the centrally-controlled Unified Shilla Kingdom, based on the king and the aristocrats in Kyŏngju, to regional clans who were developing substantial economic and military clout. Thus, in the last half of the 9th century, revolts against central authority arose in each region, with one rebel group even invading Kyŏngju and slaying the king. These struggles led to the partition of Unified Shilla power into the so-called "Later Three Kingdoms"——Later Paekche, Later Koguryŏ and Unified Shilla. Eventually, Wang Kŏn, a leader born to a clan in Later Koguryŏ, established a new unified kingdom on the Korean Peninsula. This was the Koryŏ Dynasty.

In the 9th century as powerful clans established themselves in each region, it was the Sŏn (Zen) sect that provided an empowering ideology justifying their independence. Founded in China by the Indian monk Bodhidharma, Sŏn taught people not to follow the Buddha's teachings blindly. Instead, it was important to realize that man, when enlightened, is himself a Buddha and to engage in spiritual cultivation based on this realization. Due to its unique epistemology formed through the melding of Indian Buddhism and Chinese Taoism, Sŏn has been the object of fervent faith and extensive research from its inception up to modern times. The idea that any one, when enlightened, is identical to the Buddha is highly progressive. It was this notion that eventually gave birth to the intellectual developments of the Korean Middle Ages. Breaking free from the oppressive identity between the monarch and the Buddha, members of regional clans came to believe that they too could be king.

Following the introduction of Sŏn, the center of Korean Buddhism naturally moved from Kyŏngju to outlying regions. Regional clans became devoted patrons, erecting Sŏn monasteries in each area. Later, people were to refer to this as the era of the "Nine Mountain Sŏn Schools", in reference to nine prominent Sŏn monasteries founded around this time.

From the early part of the Unified Shilla period, the kingdom had begun establishing mountain temples out of military and administrative considerations. As time went by, temples gradually were founded far away from urban areas in remote mountains. This development continued during the Koryŏ period, so that mountain temples came to be considered the authentic form of Korean temples. Within the natural environment of the Korean Peninsula, Koreans developed the aesthetic of mountain temples, which can be seen both at large monasteries founded mostly during the Unified Shilla period such as Hwaŏmsa Temple on Mt. Chirisan, Haeinsa Temple on Mt. Kayasan, Songgwangsa Temple on Mt. Chogyesan, Pusŏksa Temple on Mt. Sobaeksan and Pŏpchusa Temple on Mt. Songnisan, and at elegant temples such as Muwisa Temple at Kangjin, Pongjŏngsa Temple in Andong, Kaeshimsa Temple in Sŏsan, and Naesosa Temple in Puan. In addition to Kyŏngju, these are another source of pride for Korean culture.

Mountain temples are therefore ideal places for visitors to discover Korea's unique beauty. Even visitors to Kyŏngju should definitely take the opportunity to visit a mountain temple. If you are interested, Unmunsa Temple, situated 90 minutes by car from Kyŏngju, is probably the best place to go. The mountain path winding around a large lake is particularly beautiful. The nuns who attend the temple's seminary chant at 3 a.m. and 6 p.m. The singing of this unaccompanied female choir is imbued with a sacred atmosphere reminiscent of Gregorian chants.

In addition to Kyŏngju and Korea's mountain temples, *yangban* (aristocratic) architecture of the Chosŏn Dynasty is a representative relic of Korea's traditional culture. The artifacts most symbolic of *yangban* culture are aristocratic residences and *sŏwon* (private Confucian academies). Such *yangban* architecture has been best preserved in Andong, an area about 2 hours from Kyŏngju by car. However, for those visitors to Kyŏngju interested in experiencing Chosŏn culture, I would like to point out that it is not necessary to go all the way to Andong. Instead, I would strongly recommend Yangdong Folk Village in An'gang and Oksan Sŏwon, situated about 30 minutes from downtown Kyŏngju. Yangdong Folk Village consists of tile and thatch-roofed houses nestled together on a small hill, while Oksan Sŏwon and Tongnaktang are

UNMUNSA TEMPLE
Situated about 90 minutes by car from Kyŏngju, Unmunsa Temple boasts the charm and elegance characteristic of Koreas mountain temples. In particular, the morning and evening chanting of approximately 200 nuns is a splendid example of unaccompanied female choir music.

YANGDONG FOLK VILLAGE
Situated on the northern outskirts of Kyŏngju, this traditional village formed around 400 years ago during the Chosŏn Dynasty. This typical yangban (nobleman) village openly exhibits the Korean consciousness of living in harmony with nature and the beauty of hanok (traditional wooden houses).

situated on the edge of a valley. The location and positioning of these buildings convey a sense of serenity. Whereas mountain temples serve as places for spiritual cultivation, *yangban* residences and sŏwon demonstrate how to live everyday life in harmony with nature. Yangdong Folk Village and Oksan Sŏwon certainly will not disappoint you, for they show the extent to which Koreans have lived in an intimate relationship with their environment. Only after you have seen and experienced such places, can you rightfully claim to have seen and understood Korea.

PART 1

Pulguksa Temple

There Are No Flowers in Pulguksa Temple's Courtyard

Foundation Record of Pulguksa Temple /
Grand Master P'yohun / King Kyŏngdŏk / Temple Layout /
Explanation of Famous Artifacts at Pulguksa Temple

KOREAN CULTURAL PROPERTIES

Is there any Korean who has finished the minimum required years of schooling and still does not know about Pulguksa Temple? Probably not. There might be a few who have never been to Kyŏngju, but virtually everyone who does visit ends up going to this famous monastery. In a sense, Pulguksa Temple is the most well-known cultural treasure in Korea.

Of those who visit, how many come away thinking that the temple isn't splendid and beautiful? How many find it boring? Probably no one. In this sense, the monastery serves as a prominent cultural treasure and a symbol of Korean beauty.

Several years ago, an architectural journal conducted a survey, asking architects to name the best traditional building. Surprisingly enough, Pulguksa Temple was not even among the top five! I realize that things great and famous are sometimes objects of envy. Neglect is sometimes the price of fame. However, I had no idea that even professional architects would ignore this important monastery. I suppose I was even more disappointed since I had expected Pulguksa Temple to be the number one pick. To be honest, I think the problem lies not with the temple but with the limited perspective of many of the respondents.

According to my subjective opinion, any discussion of Korea's most representative traditional architecture would have to include monasteries. The most excellent examples would naturally include Yŏngju's Pusŏk Temple, Sunch'ŏn's Sŏnamsa Temple and Kyŏngju's Pulguksa Temple. Each of these monasteries has a unique architectural aspiration, in particular when it comes to expressing a harmonious relationship with nature. Situated next to remnants of the Paektu Taegan (the chain of mountain ridges running down the Korean Peninsula from Mt. Paektusan), Pusŏksa Temple has a majestic scale. Sŏnamsa Temple, on the other hand, is nestled within the gentle slopes of Mt. Chogyesan. Pulguksa Temple is situated on a mountain slope, yet has converted the incline into a flat area. To put it another way, Pusŏksa Temple has an excellent location while Sŏnamsa Temple excels in its use of space between buildings. Pulguksa Temple, on the other hand, is noted for the technical expertise seen in its stonework and excellent design. Due to these unique features, most Koreans prefer Pusŏksa Temple for its open and magnanimous mood, while Japanese like Sŏnamsa Temple for its profound atmosphere and Westerners like Pulguksa Temple for its manmade ingenuity.

There are many monasteries in Korea similar to the Pusŏksa and Sŏnamsa Temples. However, Pulguksa Temple is unique in the way it pursues harmony by contrasting the manmade and the natural.

FALSEHOODS OF PULGUKSA TEMPLE'S "RECORD" AND "TRACES"

There are two records dealing with Pulguksa Temple's foundation and history: The "Record of Generations of Sages Who Made Successive Constructions of Pulguksa Temple"[1] (hereafter abbreviated as the "Record") and "Traces of Pulguksa Temple"[2] (hereafter abbreviated as "Traces"). The former was written in 1740 by the Venerable Tong'ŭn, while the latter was reissued in 1708 by the Venerable Paengnyŏn. These records tell the monastery's history and even allow us to imagine how the temple must have looked during Kim Taesŏng's time. We are fortunate to have them.

Unfortunately, they contain falsehoods and mistakes. The "Record" tells the events leading up to the temple's foundation along with other stories which had been passed down. It also talks about the temple's connection with Hwaŏm (Ch. *Hua-yen*) thought. Yet as Prof. Min Yŏnggyu pointed out in his exposition on this work, these stories, whether true or not, were undoubtedly taken from somewhere else. For example, five of Ch'oe Ch'iwon's writings appear in identical passages in both the "Record" and the "History of Hwaŏm Temple on Mt. Chirisan".[3] Since "Traces" does not even get Iryŏn's birthdate right, its value as a historical document is highly suspect.

Why are these so inaccurate? Actually, this problem is not limited to the records of Pulguksa Temple. In the wake of the destructive Hideyoshi Invasions (1592-1598), each monastery worked to resurrect its traditions and authority. As temple histories and records were compiled, writers constructed ancient histories for temples where the original histories had been destroyed. (In the secular realm, a parallel trend occurred with the creation of fake genealogical records.) Before long, virtually every temple claimed to have been founded by Ado, Ŭisang, Wonhyo, or at the very least, Tosŏn.[4] In the "Record", Pulguksa Temple's foundation is pushed back to the time of King Pŏphŭng (r. 514-540). "Traces" goes even further, claiming that the temple was founded by Ado during the reign of King Nulchi (r. 417-458)! Needless to say, no scholars accept these dates.

The only thing these unsound historical documents show us is that distortions of the truth, when seen for what they are by later generations, end up being nothing more than sources of ridicule. One is reminded of the 'Peace Dam'—a senseless structure near the North Korean border that was supposedly built in order to stop the North from flooding the South. It now merely serves as another testimony to the falsehood of 20th century man.

Problems with the Theory that Kim Taesŏng Constructed the Temple

Credible historical references to the founding of Pulguksa Temple are limited to the line in the *Memorabilia of the Three Kingdoms*[5] stating that "Taesŏng demonstrated his filial piety to his parents of two lifetimes." This legend is widely known and will be more discussed later, in the first section on Sŏkpulsa Temple. At this point, I would like to repeat two short passages.

> He therefore built Pulguksa Temple for the parents of his present life, and Sŏkpulsa Temple for the parents of his previous life. He invited Shillim and P'yohun respectively to reside in the temples. ("Kohyangjŏn")

> Taesŏng, First Minister during the reign of King Kyŏngdŏk, began the construction of Pulguksa Temple in the tenth year of T'ien-pao (751). Taesŏng passed away during the reign of King Hyegong on the second day of the twelfth month in the ninth year of Tali (774). The nation thus had to finish the temple. Initially, the illustrious Yogacara monk Hangma was invited to stay at the temple, which has continued to exist to the present day. ("Temple Record"[6])

The monk Iryŏn quoted these two passages, saying that he did not know which one was correct. The interesting question for us is not which one is accurate, but how Kim Taesŏng, even in the capacity of premier, could undertake such a grand project all by himself and why the government came forward and completed his unfinished project.

In the spring of 1991, Dr. Nam Chŏnu and Prof. Shin Yŏnghun each independently proposed that the answer could be found in the "King Kyŏngdŏk" section of *Memorabilia of the Three Kingdoms*. Dr. Nam put forth this view in his book *Sŏkpulsa Temple*,[7] which was published on April 20, 1991, by Ilchogak. Shin Yŏnghun presented his view during the

'Issues of Sŏkkuram' Conference held at the Academy of Korean Studies on May 3, 1991. Just as Dr. Nam had done, Shin claimed that the *Memorabilia of the Three Kingdoms* passage about King Kyŏngdŏk's prayer for a child was associated with the foundation of Pulguksa Temple.

THE STORY OF HOW KING KYŎNGDŎK HAD A SON

It is said that when Heaven gives good fortune to man, it does not give him everything. In this sense, life is said to be fair. As ruler during the heyday of Unified Shilla culture, King Kyŏngdŏk was a fortunate man; but he unfortunately had no son. He therefore went to the highly competent Grand Master P'yohun and asked him to intercede on his behalf. Iryŏn, using his uniquely symbolic writing style, opens his account with the following, rather shocking, sentence.

King Kyŏngdŏk's jade stick [male organ] was eight *ch'on* long, and he had no son. He therefore cast out the queen and took Lady Manwol in her place... She was Premier Ŭichung's daughter.

According to the Japanese surveyor Yoneda Miyoji, the *cha* (Korean foot) in use when Pulguksa Temple was built was 29.7cm long, which would mean that the king's 'jade stick' would have been 23.76cm long. In a recent 'sexology' article in *DongA Ilbo* ("Namsŏng ŭi him", January 1, 1996), there were statistics on the size of the sexual organs of different animals. The average length of an adult male's erection was 15cm, and was 11.2cm for Korean males. (For your information, a whale's erection is 3m long, that of a horse 1m, and that of a mosquito 0.03cm.) In other words, the king's 'jade stick' was twice as long as the average man's.

According to Shin, the king's inability to have a son was *because* his male organ was so long. In other words, there was something wrong with him. Nam, on the other hand, interprets this to mean, "*Although* he had a male organ eight inches long," meaning that there was no problem on the male side. I really respect Iryŏn as a great monk. Even though he was ordained, he did not hesitate to begin his account like this. He continues as follows:

One day, the king told the Venerable P'yohun, "Lacking good fortune, I have been unable to have a son. Would the Venerable One ask the High Emperor [the highest deity] to give me a son? P'yohun ascended to the Heavenly Emperor and told him. He later returned with the message. "He says that the king may have a daughter but cannot have a son." The king told him, "I would be satisfied if the daughter were changed into a son." P'yohun went back up to heaven and told the High Emperor, who informed him, "The king may have a son, but this will mean danger for his kingdom."

As P'yohun was about to descend, the High Emperor added, "The distinction between Heaven and Earth must not be disturbed. Yet you frequently go back and forth as if visiting a neighboring village. By doing so, you disturb the functioning of Heaven. You must not come here any more."

P'yohun returned and gave the message to the king, who replied, "Though the kingdom be endangered, I would like to have a son to succeed me." Later, when Empress Manwol bore him a son, the king was overjoyed.

When the prince was eight years old, the king died and the prince therefore ascended the throne. This was the Great King Hyegong. Since the prince was young, the queen managed political affairs; yet the affairs of state did not go smoothly. Bandits appeared like swarms of bees, until no one could stop them. Thus P'yohun's words turned out to be true.

Since the king was a girl who had been born as a boy, he spent the time from his first birthday until his ascension to the throne engaged solely in women's pursuits. He liked to carry a silk pouch and jest with sages. The kingdom thus entered a period of crisis until the king was finally assassinated by Kim Yangsang, who became King Sŏndŏk.

After P'yohun, no more holy men appeared in Shilla.

King Kyŏngdŏk's Rule and the 'Cultured President'

King Kyŏngdŏk (r. 742-765) was the 'art monarch', who oversaw the blossoming of Unified Shilla culture. In a sense, he was the 'cultured President' that we're always dreaming of these days. Indeed, outstanding art works of the Unified Shilla period were all produced during his reign. Masterpieces from this period include Pulguksa Temple, Sŏkpulsa Temple (Sŏkkuram), the Sŏkka and Tabo Pagodas, Emille Bell, many of the stone Buddha figures on Kyŏngju's Mt. Namsan and the flat Buddha figures unearthed at Anapchi—in short, most of the remarkable statues and Buddhist relics housed in the National Museum. Although they disappeared long ago, the giant Hwangnyongsa Temple bell and the standing Medicine Buddha from Punhwangsa Temple were also produced at this time. In short, King Kyŏngdŏk ruled for the third quarter of the eighth century that marked the height of Shilla's effulgence.

Unfortunately, this was also to be the last blossoming of Unified Shilla culture. The 100 years of cultural development that the kingdom enjoyed after unification ended with King Kyŏngdŏk's reign. As soon as the king died and his son assumed the throne, the aristocrats immediately set out to undermine the absolute power of the monarch. In the end, King Hyegong was killed by one of his ministers, who then assumed the throne. In the years that followed, Unified Shilla was a different society characterized by endless feuds among aristocratic factions vying for power. For this reason, Kim Pushik in his historical work *Historical Records of the Three Kingdoms*[8] uses the terms 'middle' and 'late' Shilla, so as to differentiate clearly between the periods before and after King

Kyŏngdŏk's demise.

In history, this phenomena occurs so frequently that it would appear to be a principle of cultural history. During the Koryŏ period, the civil aristocrats developed a flourishing culture that peaked during the third quarter of the twelfth century. King Ŭijong ruled for this period during which all the famous masterpieces of inlay celadon were produced. However, Ŭijong was overthrown by a *coup d'etat*, which led to massive changes in Koryŏ's aristocratic culture.

This same transformation occurred during the Chosŏn Dynasty. During the fourth quarter of the 18th century, King Chŏngjo ruled during the entire literary and artistic renaissance, but after his sudden death, the period of powerful families ensued, eventually leading to an inevitable decline in culture. Along a similar vein, Heinrich Wölfflin compared the Renaissance with baroque art. He put forth a basic principle of art history when he mused, "The mountain called the Renaissance is a rugged peak where one doesn't have the time to stop and smoke even a single bowl of tobacco."

King Kyŏngdŏk may have sensed the restlessness and danger lurking behind the scenes during the kingdom's cultural golden age. As mentioned in the *Memorabilia of the Three Kingdoms* and confirmed by historical research, King Kyŏngdŏk was aware that the absolute power of the monarchy was being challenged by the power of aristocrats. In order to strengthen the fragile monarchy, the king reformed the government bureaucracy and constructed the great Emille Bell to glorify his father, King Sŏngdŏk, who had established the framework for a strong monarchy. In order to obtain a son, he also undertook a large Buddhist project. As ancient kings had done before him and numerous dictators have done since, the king undertook massive construction projects in order to promote his authority and ward off challenges from aristocrats and the common people. Of course, he had to undertake projects that went beyond any previous undertakings. Needless to say, such excessive

SŎKKA PAGODA
Consisting of three stories atop
a two-story base, this structure with its
perfect design, represents the acme of
Unified Shilla pagodas.

projects ultimately weakened the kingdom. The fact that Premier (i.e., prime minister) Kim Taesŏng personally acted as supervisor shows how the project was given top priority.

In the end, none of King Kyŏngdŏk's dreams was realized. In order to strengthen the monarchy, he was in dire need of a son, but in the end, his son died at the hands of the aristocrats. The king's repeated attempts to cast the 'Divine Bell of King Sŏngdŏk' failed, and the work was left for his son to complete in the seventh year of his reign (771). Unable to complete Pulguksa Temple, he also left this to his son. Do these projects indicate that the kingdom during King Kyŏngdŏk's reign was powerful but later went into decline? Or should we assume that these projects themselves brought on the decline? (Or was it perhaps due to the influence of celestial deities?) At any rate, the kingdom's culture had gradually blossomed then suddenly declined, and Pulguksa Temple was established at the apex of this parabola.

THERE ARE NO FLOWER BEDS IN THE PULGUKSA TEMPLE COURTYARD

Temples after the Three Kingdoms period were built using a number of popular designs, but the layout of Pulguksa Temple is one of a kind, giving the temple a definite distinctiveness and charm.

Early Korean temples were built on flat areas within cities. Examples include the Chŏngamsa, Chŏngnimsa and Hwangnyongsa Temple sites, respectively situated in P'yŏng'yang, Puyŏ and Kyŏngju. In Kyŏngju's Kuhwang-dong (Nine Emperors Village)—the downtown section of Sŏrabŏl—there were nine temples that had the character *hwang* (emperor) in their names. These included Hwangnyongsa, Punhwangsa and Hwangboksa Temple. At this point, I'm sure someone will ask me what nine monasteries were doing in a single area. To this, my response would be that, one day in Seoul's Taech'i-dong, I saw ten churches in the shopping area of a single apartment complex.

During this period, most temples were in the city and most had

GALLERIES In all temples, galleries emphasize authority and order. They may represent strict adherence to monastic discipline or the monarchy's protection of its subjects.

hoerang. These long walkways or galleries were covered by roofs which were supported by evenly spaced pillars. They often had a single wall with windows and occasional doors. These galleries clearly defined the boundary between the sacred and the secular. Moreover, since the king was identified with the Buddha, the temple where the Buddha was enshrined was modeled after the king's residence. Since the palace had galleries, monasteries had them. In later times, only halls such as the Main Buddha Hall or Paradise Hall were thought to be the sacred area of the Buddha, but in these early times, the entire area of the temple inside the galleries was thought to be holy. The temple's wooden pagoda housed the sarira (jewel-like remains) of the Buddha and was therefore an object of worship. To give such a sacred object due precedence, no other decorations or sculptures were built next to it.

In the Middle Shilla period, 'mountain temples' (*san-sa*), such as the ten Hwaŏmsa temples built by Ŭisang, were founded in each region of the kingdom. These temples no longer had galleries, perhaps because the mountainous terrain surrounding the temples performed the galleries' delimitative function. During the Later Shilla period, the Nine Mountain Sŏn (Zen) monasteries were founded in remote regions of the kingdom. In the new Buddhist movement that ensued, the openness of Sŏn took precedence over the strict observances of the Doctrinal Schools (Kyo). The strict order and boundaries implied by the galleries were thus deemed unnecessary. The marvel of nature and a relaxed ambiance were more in keeping with this new trend. Thus courtyards landscaped with trees and flowerbeds replaced the galleries. With these changes, monasteries, which had previously occupied level areas in cities, gradually moved into the mountains.

However, Pulguksa Temple does not belong to either of these city or mountain temple styles. Although it is situated on the slopes of Mt. T'ohamsan, the temple is designed as if it were on flat ground. It was not built as a Sŏn monastery, but rather as a Doctrinal monastery representing the universe as seen by the Hwaŏm (Flower Garland) School. Its construction was an earthly representation of the realm of the Buddha. For this reason, the temple has galleries but no flowers or trees in the courtyard. Moreover, in order to reduce the mountain slope to a flat area, a giant stone embankment had to be constructed. These are the most distinguishing and beautiful features of the temple.

THE BEAUTY OF PULGUKSA TEMPLE'S STONEWORK

Anyone visiting Pulguksa Temple is immediately impressed by the walls of stacked stone. Iryŏn, when describing the stonework of the 'cloud bridges' tersely claimed that there was no other temple in the east like it. During the late Chosŏn Dynasty, the romantic writer Pak Chong in his essay "A Trip to the Eastern Capital"[9] [Kyŏngju], exclaimed that its design was "peculiar and magnificent".

When I guide visitors from foreign art galleries, every one of them invariably stops in front of the stonework at the entrance to the temple and exclaims that it is "wonderful" or "fantastic". Indeed, this stonework was the main reason that it took 24 years to complete the construction of the temple.

The stonework, 300 *cha* (about 90 meters) in total length, leaves a brilliant impression due to its elaborate design. Although one might expect such complexity to be distracting, just the opposite is the case: looking at the stacked stones, one is filled with a sense of calm. As it says in the *History of Chosŏn Architecture*,[10] "A close inspection reveals that, of the stonework's two levels, the lower level is made of natural stone while the upper one is made using artificially cut and shaped stones. In this sense, the lower serves as an expression of natural beauty while the upper one demonstrates manmade beauty. It is thus simple, yet has variation, and this variation purposefully shows a progression from natural to manmade beauty." Ernest F. Fenollosa once praised a pair of pagodas at Yakushi Temple in Nara, Japan, as a 'frozen melody'. I think of Pulguksa Temple's stonework as the moment when the melody climaxes in an opera's finale.

The stone wall is basically made up of rectangular stone blocks that have been stacked in rows. As an exquisite expression of manmade beauty, the Blue Cloud, White Cloud, Lotus Flower and Seven Gems Bridges (Chŏngŭn'gyo, Paegun'gyo, Yŏnhwagyo and Chilbogyo) are made up of rectangular stones, with the hidden portions filled in with tightly packed natural stones. Uncut stones of various dimensions were freely used for the foundations. Using the *kŭraeng'i* technique of traditional architecture, the bottom surfaces of the rectangular stone blocks have been carved to fit the uneven upper surface of the natural stones. By doing so, the cut stones can be used without damaging the natural stones beneath them. These even rows of stone lead up to the

STONEWORK AND THE BLUE CLOUD AND WHITE CLOUD BRIDGES
This stone substructure was built to transform a
mountain slope into a level area. Symbolically, the
staircases ('bridges') represent the path into the Buddha Land.
The stonework also demonstrates the ancient
Korean aesthetic which sought a synthesis between
the natural and the man-made.

elegant stonework supporting Pŏmyŏngnu (Floating Reflection Pavilion). Ch'oe Sunu, in his paper "Pulguksa Temple's Large Stone Platform",[11] describes the stonework as follows:

> This stone platform consists of large and small natural stones and exquisitely carved rectangular stone blocks. These have been stacked in a spontaneous fashion so as to accord with the general rhythm of the whole. I'm breathless as I witness Shilla's mysterious sense of harmony between stability and rhythm and between the natural and the artificial.

> My favorite part of Pulguksa Temple's stonework is the natural-stone staircase below the Floating Reflection Pavilion. Looking at its large, dignified pillars so exquisitely-fashioned, one seems to hear the world's first breath, an unselfish harmony. This world is filled with many nations and peoples, but who among them can take such frightfully ugly [actually, beautiful] stones and use them, without modification, to make such an appealing stone structure?

PULGUKSA TEMPLE'S SYMBOLISM

At this point, we no longer know the exact master plan of Pulguksa Temple. Yet, from the existing buildings and analysis of the "Record", we are able to ascertain the basic outlines of its design. These days, we look at the temple from the standpoint of a tourist and see it as a beautiful example of ancient architecture. But at the time it was built, it was truly meant to be an architectural manifestation of the realm of the Buddha. This spirit can be found in each minor element, whether it be a stone or a door.

This point holds true for all religious architecture. In the Middle Ages in the West, the floor space of cathedrals was shaped like a cross. The Greek cross was symmetrical, whereas the Latin cross was vertically taller.

The most representative structure with floor space in the shape of a Greek cross is the Ayasofya (Hagia Sophia) in Constantinople (modern-day Istanbul). A horizontal version of the Latin cross, on the other hand, became the basis for Romanesque cathedrals. In decorations from the entrance of the church up to the altar, this symbolism of the cross was very elaborate. There is no time to go into this anymore at this point, but I would like to say there have been art historians such as Erwin Panofsky who were masters at interpreting Western iconography. In the hopes that such a master might appear in Korea, I will now introduce the basic symbolism behind Pulguksa Temple's architecture. While this might strike the reader as unfamiliar and a bit boring, I would recommend reading on, with at least the idea of developing patience. This knowledge is, after all, essential if one is to understand Pulguksa Temple properly.

The stone staircase in front of Pulguksa Temple is the entrance to the celestial spheres, at the top of which stands Mt. Sumerusan (represented by the Floating Reflection Pavilion). For this reason, the "Record" refers to the pavilion as the Sumi Pŏmjonggak (Sumeru Bell Tower). It is said that 108 people can sit within the pavilion (108 signifying the traditional enumeration of mental defilements in Buddhism). The Blue Cloud and White Cloud 'Bridges' (staircases) together have 33 steps, representing the Trayatrimsa (Heaven of the Thirty-three). Texts disagree on the staircases' names. The "Record" lists the upper one as the Blue Cloud Bridge and the lower one as the White Cloud Bridge. "A Trip to the Eastern Capital" follows suit, but says that, to be exact, the rainbow-shaped arch at the top of the first flight of steps is the White Cloud Bridge and that the point at the top of the second staircase where it crosses over to Chahamun (the Purple Mist Gate) is the Blue Cloud Bridge. I don't know if this is correct but, at any rate, the Blue Cloud Bridge is on top and the White Cloud Bridge on bottom.

After climbing up through the Heaven of the Thirty-three and passing through Chahamun, one comes face to face with the Taeungjŏn (Main

Buddha Hall), where the Buddha is enshrined. On both sides, one finds the Sŏkka and Tabo Pagodas, standing as if they were two attendants. These two structures are the exact architectural expressions of a line from the "Looking at Jeweled Pagodas" section of the *Lotus Sutra*. According to this scripture, when Tabo (Many Jewels) Buddha was a Bodhisattva in training, he made the following vow: "After becoming a Buddha [i.e., attaining enlightenment] and passing away, may I rise out of the ground as a stupa in any place where someone is expounding the *Lotus Sutra* and bear testimony, saying 'This is indeed a good thing.'" Later, when the Buddha was expounding the truth of the *Lotus Sutra*, a pagoda adorned with the Seven Precious Gems (gold, silver, lapis lazuli, crystal, agate, ruby and jade) suddenly came forth from the ground. This is the story behind the Tabo Pagoda, and it explains why this stone structure is so elaborate.

This episode involving the Tabo Buddha and Sakyamuni is also depicted by two Buddha statues sitting next to each other. For this reason, the two jeweled-remains found in the structure's sarira receptacle are quite possibly the remains of both Tabo and Sakyamuni.

To the west of the Main Buddha Hall lies the separate Kŭngnakchŏn (Paradise Hall). Amitabha Buddha, the enlightened being who watches over the Paradise of the West, is enshrined here. The Seven Gems Bridge (Ch'ilbogyo) and the Lotus Flower Bridge (Yŏnhwagyo) are the names of the two staircases that lead up to Anyangmun (Tranquility Development Gate). The Seven Gems Bridge is a staircase with depictions of the Seven Precious Gems carved on each step. Although the engravings are now almost completely rubbed away, Pak Chong, in his work "A Trip to the Eastern Capital", says that he could clearly see them. However, the lotus blossom designs on the Lotus Flower Bridge are still clearly visible. Thus the path to paradise was decorated with the Seven Precious Gems and lotus blossoms. Behind the Paradise Hall, there are three staircases, each with 16 steps. Together, these add up to 48 and represent the 48 vows that Amitabha took when he was a Bodhisattva in training. As a result of these vows, he created the Western Paradise in order to help living beings.

This symbolism continues at Pirojŏn (Vairocana Hall) and Kwanŭmjŏn (Avalokitesvara Hall), but I am unable to go into this fully. My aim here is not to discuss the significance of each aspect of the temple, but merely to prove that the builders did indeed employ a symbolic structure in their master plan.

THE MATHEMATICAL HARMONY OF PULGUKSA TEMPLE

Even though Pulguksa Temple has a grand symbolism, this would be nothing if it did not have the proper layout to support it. Without a precise design, the symbols would have been a failure in both the artistic and the architectural sense. Coomaraswami, a friend of Panofsky and an occasional collaborator on the latter's iconographic studies, says in his book *Dance of Siva*, "The Art without science is nothing." In this work, he stressed the importance of harmony based on mathematical relationships. Pulguksa Temple, just like nearby Sŏkpulsa Temple, was constructed based on precise mathematical proportions. Analysis of the numerical distances as given by the surveyor Yoneda has been presented on the diagram. The numbers referred to here represent proportional relationships and are the basis for the structure's harmony and symmetry.

To explain the diagram, if one takes half the distance between the Tabo and Sŏkka Pagodas as representing a unit of measurement, one finds that the buildings within the temple complex have all been positioned at multiples of this unit. For example, the galleries running east to west are four times as wide, while those running north to south are five times as long. The center of the Buddha Hall's northern (rear) wall is at the point of an equilateral triangle four times as long. That is to say, if one drew a line from Kyŏng-nu (Sutra Pavilion) to Chong-nu (Belfry) and used this as one side of an equilateral triangle, the other two sides would meet at

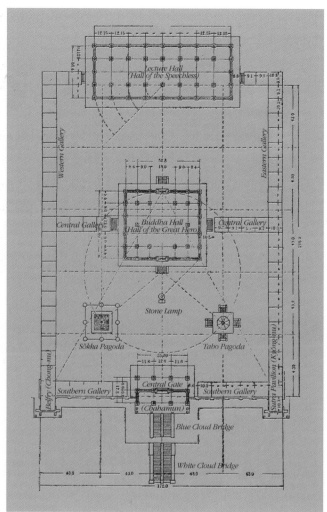

the back of the Buddha Hall. In addition, if one used the steps in front of the Buddha Hall as a central point for a circle running through both the Sŏkka and Tabo Pagodas, the other side of the circle would touch the center of the Buddha Hall's back wall.

The Buddha Hall, Sŏkka Pagoda and Tabo Pagoda are all equidistant from each other with the stone lantern in the middle, while the height of the Buddha Hall's roof and the distance from the Buddha Hall to Chahamun are at a 1:2 ratio. If one draws a circle from the Sŏkka

Pagoda, with a radius equal to the pagoda's height, the circle covers all the space in the Buddha Hall's courtyard.

The buildings' floor spaces are also set in proportional relationships according to this hypothetical unit. On the Sŏkka and Tabo Pagodas, the base stones of the first levels are as wide as 1/3 of the unit, while the spaces between the front pillars of the lecture hall are 2/5 of the unit (this being equal to 1/5 of a diagonal across a square with 1-unit-long sides).

The width of the Sŏkka and Tabo Pagodas' lower bases is 1/3 the width of the Buddha Hall, while the floor space of the Sŏkka Pagoda is 1/10 that of the Buddha Hall.

The above measurements prove that the temple's builders set up a standard unit of measurement. While using this in the form of multiples, they also created measurements using diagonals (both whole and dissected). In this way, they could easily show quantitative relationships between various structures. Due to these subtle proportional relationships, Pulguksa Temple has a grandeur not found at other temples.

A Detailed Look at Pulguksa Temple's Architecture

We are now ready to look at some of the individual historic relics at Pulguksa Temple. Unfortunately, there is not enough space here to do so. Among the temple's artifacts, we find Sŏkka Pagoda, Tabo Pagoda, stone lantern, worship stone, gilt seated-Amitabha statue, gilt seated-Vairocana statue and Kwanghak Stupa. Each of these is a national treasure that cannot be properly covered in anything shorter than a chapter. I will thus limit myself to discussing some of the hidden beauty that the first-time visitor is likely to miss.

I often show visitors around Kyŏngju. In particular, I try to fulfill my obligations as an advocate of Korean art, by volunteering to guide visitors from foreign museums. After all, if they leave with a strong impression of Korea, their attitude toward the 'Korea room' in their museum is likely to change. At this point, I would like to share some of the exquisite architectural details that I always include on this tour. When Mr. and Mrs. James Wood came from the Chicago Institute of Art one spring, I took them on this exact course.

First, I would like to point out the slightly receding levels on the stone staircase in front of the Buddha Hall. The curving line reminds one of an upturned collar or the end of a loose sleeve. I'm amazed when I think back on these ancient builders—how they instilled such joy and loveliness in these sharp, yet gentle, contours. When I pulled Mr. Wood over to look at this, he repeatedly shook his head while repeating, "Unbelievable!"

Secondly, I would like to point out the use of straight lines on the Sŏkka Pagoda's upturned eaves. While people tend to look carefully at the Tabo Pagoda's elaborate structure, they are usually content with just a general impression of the Sŏkka Pagoda. This pagoda's charm comes from its upturned roof stones. Yet, if one looks closely, the lines on the

RECESSED LINES ON THE STAIRS LEADING UP TO THE BUDDHA HALL
One can only marvel at the sculptors who took the time to add this recession. With its lovely curve, it looks like a jacket collar.

roof ridges are actually straight. The eaves project straight downward but as they reach the corners, a thick lip has been added. When seen from the bottom, the roof therefore appears to be curving upward. In other words, an optical illusion has been used to create the impression of a curve. The Sŏkka Pagoda's beauty lies in this detail work which gives it a sense of gentle elegance combined with firm strength.

The third such interesting detail can be found where the carved stone blocks rest on natural stone. The bottom of the cut stones has been carved to fit snugly with the contours of the natural stone underneath. Foreigners who see this for the first time can't believe their eyes. They gain a whole new appreciation for the effort and planning that went into the reconciliation between the natural and the manmade. And they are especially impressed when they see the stone wall on the western side of Paradise Hall. Here, the path beside the hall gently slopes upward. In the long stone foundation, vertically-placed stonework projects from the wall's midsection. However, the line of these vertical pieces gradually

STONEWORK USING THE 'KŬRAENG'I' TECHNIQUE
Instead of cutting the natural stone, the rectangular stones above have been cut to fit the contours of the natural stones below. In wooden architecture, this is known as the 'kŭraeng'i' technique. It is seen only in Korea.

STONE FOUNDATION ON THE WESTERN SIDE OF THE PARADISE HALL *The horizontal line separating the upper and lower sections of this stone wall has been exquisitely designed so that it gradually rises with the slope.*

curves upward along with the upward incline of the path—a fascinating innovation that gives the structure a dynamic feeling. In the wall's midsection, the use of long blocks of cut stone which jut out like wooden beams is another interesting idea. After my tour of Kyŏngju with Mr. Wood, I asked him to name the thing that most impressed him. He paused for moment, saying it was a difficult question, but finally chose the stonework on the west side of Paradise Hall.

Fourth, I would like to point out the lotus patterns carved in the steps below Anyangmun of Paradise Hall. Although they seem more or less distinct according to season, angle and lighting, they are definitely visible even to an 'earthly eye'. When Mr. Wood's eyes lit upon these, he was deeply impressed.

Fifth, I would like to suggest walking up to Avalokitesvara Hall and looking southward over the tile and mud wall at the galleries and Tabo

Pagoda. From this angle, one can sense the peaceful atmosphere found in temples with galleries.

The sixth exquisite detail work can be found on the stone fragments lying on the open lot to the west of the temple. Although previously part of the temple, these were discarded during the temple's restorations. While anyone would recognize the old foundation stones, one might miss the interesting stone with an oval hole in the middle. This was used in the temple's outhouse. Next to this, there is a complete toilet. Contrary to what one would expect, the stonework on this piece has been exquisitely designed. When the museum director Mr. Wood saw this, he asked why this had been carved so much more elaborately than the others. Off the cuff, I told him it was probably "For Director only". Laughing at the remark, he said that if I wrote a book on humor, it would be a best-seller.

Strangely enough, there is also a square stone with a hollowed-out area shaped like a willow leaf and a small hole in its lower section. It is not

LOTUS PATTERNS CARVED ON THE LOTUS FLOWER BRIDGE
If one looks closely, one can see lotus designs carved on each step of this staircase. Depictions of the Seven Precious Gems are said to have been carved on Seven Gems Bridge, but even the faint outline has long since disappeared.

STONEWORK FOR THE TOILET *This splendidly crafted stonework was used for the temple's toilet. It is not clear what the hollowed-out, leaf-shaped stone was used for. Perhaps it was an 8th-century bidet.*

clear what this was used for. As it is shaped like a hospital bed pan, Shin Yŏnghun conjectured that it was an indoor flush toilet and was probably for women. At first, I agreed with this idea. But after looking it over several times, it occurred to me that it may instead have been used to collect water and wash one's rear after going to the toilet. When Mr. Wood was here, he stared for a long time at this piece before finally asking me what it was. In my scanty English, the only phrase I could come up with was "eighth century bidet". Instead of his normal response of "Really?" or some equivalent, he patted me lightly on the shoulder and chuckled, telling me, "You win."

One thing that you would not want to miss is the outhouse on the other side of the small Ilgakmun (One Enlightenment Gate). I don't mention this as a restroom to use, but as an ideal vantage point from which to look at Pulguksa Temple's *kang'wŏn* (seminary) in the distance. For those who have visited Korea's numerous mountain temples, the view will be familiar. However, since the Pulguksa temple was designed as a flat monastery with galleries, such a tranquil scene like a mountain temple gives an added air of warmth and grandeur. As we finish our tour, this serves as a good lingering impression.

When Mr. Wood looked over at the seminary nestled within the distant pines, he exclaimed in astonishment, "I have visited countless countries throughout the world, but I have never seen a country where nature plays such an important role in art and architecture." I turned to him and said, "It's only a preview."

When it comes to appreciating cultural sites, I have always said that there are beginning, middle and high level tours, and Pulguksa Temple is naturally lower level. That is not to say that neophytes will enjoy only the tours for beginners and so on. To the contrary, beginners often want to go on middle-level courses, while middle level tourists will be enchanted by beginning-level courses. On the other hand, one must attain the higher level of cultural awareness before one can comprehend the true merit of a beginner's course. This progress and cycle of return is perhaps a part of the vicissitudes and wonder of life. In this sense, an exploration of Korean culture both begins and ends at Pulguksa Temple.

June 1997

1. "Pulguksa kogŭm yŏktae chehyŏn kyech'anggi".
2. "Pulguksa sajŏk".
3. "Chirisan hwaŏmsa sajŏk".
4. Ado was the monk credited with bringing Buddhism to Shilla; Ŭisang was a renowned Hwaŏm master of the Shilla period; Wonhyo was one of the most famous monks and Buddhist scholars of the Shilla period; and Tosŏn (827-898) was famous for his writings on geomancy.
5. *Samguk yusa*.
6. "Sajunggi".
7. *Sŏkpulsa*.
8. *Samguk sagi*.
9. "Tonggyŏng kihaeng".
10. *Chosŏn kŏnch'uksa*, vol. I, 1993.
11. "Pulguksa taesŏkdan", *Muryangsujŏn paehŭllim kidung'e kidae sŏsŏ* (Seoul: Hak-ko-je, 1984).

What Did You Trust?

Disappearance of the Tabo Pagoda's Stone Lions /
Recovery of the Kwanghak Stupa / The Broken Sokka Pagoda /
The Excavation of the Sarira Reliquary / An Upset Harmony

PULGUKSA TEMPLE'S ORDEALS

If it wasn't the wrath of God, it was His jealousy. Just as the 20th century saw Mt. T'ohamsan's Sŏkpulsa Temple dissected piece by piece to be 'restored' as an invalid, Pulguksa Temple, from the time of the Japanese occupation to the Third Republic, went through numerous ordeals. These days, visitors wander through the temple, unaware that anything is amiss. So I will clench my teeth again and attempt to set down the recent history of this great world treasure. These calamities would have to be attributed to God's jealousy of the temple's perfect beauty or Heaven's anger at our blindness. Many events offer no other explanation.

Our final glimpse of the temple's past glory in the "Record" or "Traces" is when King Chŏngjo gave the temple a gift in 1796. The last mention of the temple in an old record of any kind occurs with the repair of Pirojŏn (Vairocana Hall) in 1805. We therefore have no record telling us the condition of the monastery during the 19th century. As Korea fell into misfortune, large monasteries throughout the nation also went into decline. All we know at this point is that some monks continued to reside at these large monastic complexes, unable to do anything to stop

PULGUKSA TEMPLE IN RUINS
The temple's stonework survived the Mongol and Hideyoshi Invasions, but was falling apart around the beginning of the 20th century.

the deterioration.

Pulguksa Temple reappears in the history books at the beginning of the 20th century. In August 1902, Sekino Tadasu, an assistance professor at Tokyo Imperial University, came to Korea to conduct a survey of Korea's ancient architecture. At this time, he surveyed Pulguksa Temple and took pictures. When he came, there were only a couple of monks living at the temple. Even back when "A Trip to the Eastern Capital"[1] was written, Pak Chong stated that, "Although only one among ten items remains, it is extraordinary and beautiful." In other words, only the pagodas and stupas had maintained their previous glory. These remaining artifacts caught the attention of the Japanese.

Sekino's survey was published two years later in 1904 as the *Survey Report on Korean Architecture.*[2] He sent this book to a Japanese benefactor living in Kaesŏng. This information led to the theft of one of the site's treasures. In 1906, one year after the signing of the Protectorate Treaty of 1905, the so-called Kwanghak (Bright Learning) Stupa (presently designated as Treasure No. 61) was smuggled to Japan.

Subsequent events are recorded in detail in Yi Kuyŏl's work *History of the Ordeals Suffered by Korean Cultural Properties.*[3] The full particulars of the story are as follows.

How the Kwanghak Stupa was Returned

After the Kwanghak Stupa was taken to Japan, it was set up in a restaurant by the name of Seiyoken in Tokyo's Ueno Park. Around this time, the magazine *Kokka* commissioned Sekino to write an article explaining the stupa. In 1909, Sekino returned to Korea to do further surveys of ancient sites. At this time, he asked the Government-General of Korea to return the stupa to its original site. By this time, however, the stupa could no longer be found as it had been sold to someone else. Nevertheless, Sekino tenaciously kept looking for it. In May 1933, it was finally located, two decades after being lost. The stupa was standing in the garden of a Mr. Nagao, the president of a pharmaceutical company in Tokyo. With little choice, Nagao presented the stupa as a 'gift' to the Government-General, and the stupa was thus brought back to Pulguksa Temple in July 1933.

From the Korean standpoint, the repatriation of the stupa was of course very fortunate, but why did Sekino, a citizen of Japan, work so zealously for the stupa's return? There are two possible explanations. The first is his conscience as a scholar. As an archaeologist, he was expected to promote a pro-colonial view of history. At the same time, he was a respected member of Japanese academia. At the very least, he knew that historical artifacts were supposed to be preserved *in situ* whenever possible. Second, the stupa was actually an asset under the jurisdiction of the Government-General. At this time, the Japanese colonial government thought of everything in Korea as belonging to Japan. Whether something was on the 'inland' (Japan) or the 'peninsula' (Korea), it was considered to be a property of the Japanese government. The Pulguksa Temple artifact was recovered simply because it belonged to the

*THE KWANGHAK STUPA
A superb carving with
an exquisite design,
this stupa was spirited
off to Japan but later
recovered. It serves as
just one example of the
looting of Korean
cultural treasures.*

Government-General of Korea. If the Japanese had known that the occupation would last only 36 years, rather than seek the stupa's return, they would have taken every artifact they laid eyes on back to Japan. In this case, Japan's assumption that Korea would be their colony forever turned out to be a blessing in disguise.

WHAT ABOUT THE TABO PAGODA'S STONE LIONS AND SARIRA RELIQUARY?

When Sekino went to Kyŏngju in 1909, he discovered that two of the four stone lions that had originally stood on the four corners of the Tabo pagoda's base were missing. According to Sekino, the two that had disappeared were in the best condition.

At present, there are those who attribute the theft to the Japanese man from Kaesŏng who took the Kwanghak Stupa to Japan. Others believe that Resident-General Sone Arasuke took them, along with the Sŏkpulsa Temple's marble stupa, during his first tour of inspection to Kyŏngju. It is now impossible to identify the culprit, and the stone lions have yet to be found.

To make matters worse, one of the two remaining lions (again, the one in better condition) was also stolen, although it is not clear when this happened. Since Kimura, who worked as chief scribe in what was then Kyŏngju County, stated in his 1924 writing "Growing Old in Korea",[4] "My one wish before dying is to see the pair of lions from the Tabo Pagoda returned so that the central shrine is once more complete," we can assume that the third lion was stolen after this time. At any rate, due to a scar on its face, the last lion still stands in its original position, guarding the pagoda. As the philosopher Chuang-tsu once said, "only the gnarled pine is left uncut to protect the tomb, and only the worthless willow is allowed to become an old tree."

In 1924, the Japanese colonial government conducted a major restoration of Pulguksa Temple. This project included the restoration of the stonework and staircases, repair of the Main Buddha Hall and the complete dismantling of the Tabo Pagoda. Apparently, there were no photos or records kept, or at least none have appeared so far. Due to this lack of records, those who carried out the 1970 restoration had an extremely difficult time figuring out how the temple's original design had been altered during the 1924 restoration. This knowledge was essential to restore the temple according to its original plan. If those working on the 1924 project had simply taken a few pictures or had drawn up a blueprint of the temple before their alterations, reconstructing the original design would have been an easy task.

As a result of the 1924 restoration, Pulguksa Temple was prevented from falling to ruin. However, the galleries disappeared, leaving Pŏmyŏngnu (Floating Reflection Pavilion) standing by itself in the desolate atmosphere. Although I haven't come across any photos, I'm sure that our parents and grandparents must have taken shots of the temple when they went to Kyŏngju on school field trips.

The Tabo Pagoda suffered the greatest damage during the 1924 restoration, but there isn't a single project report mentioning it. At this time, the pagoda almost surely contained a sarira reliquary, but this disappeared without a trace. But as they say, "There is no such thing as a perfect crime." On June 9, 1924, Takeuchi, the supervisor of the 1924 construction, sent an official statement to the Kyŏngju County Governor. Known as the "Official Notification for Transference of Discovered Items", the statement included the following:

> With regard to the disposal of the two Buddha figures discovered when repairing the Tabo Pagoda, the chief of the Educational Bureau has asked that they be sent to be examined. We are therefore sending them to the Religious Affairs Office in Kyŏngbok Palace. (Quoted from the *Pulguksa Temple Restoration Report* produced by the Office of Cultural Properties in 1976).

We know that two Buddha images were discovered in the pagoda at Hwangboksa Temple in Kyŏngju. It appears that such images were also enshrined in the Tabo Pagoda. However, no one knows what these images looked like or where they disappeared to. They may well have been masterpieces comparable to the sarira reliquary in the Sŏkka Pagoda.

It has been said that during the restoration in 1924, the Japanese replaced some of the natural stone from the stonework with artificially cut blocks. As a result, the stonework, which had originally demonstrated the harmony between the natural and the manmade, took on an artificial

air. Japanese workers who had heard ensuing criticism critical of this 'Japanese' charge broke off the squared corners of the stones with hammers to give them a more 'natural' look. It appears that the Japanese are never satisfied until they have completely transformed an object. In many cases, their 'naturalness' is a forced naturalness or, one might say, a contrived naturalness.

In this condition, Pulguksa Temple weathered two more decades of the Japanese occupation, the Liberation, the Korean War, the April 19 Revolution and the May 16 *coup d'etat* without any major mishap. Then in September 1966, the newspapers reported that the Sŏkka Pagoda had been shaked during an earthquake. This event led to an incident that was to put the pagoda in the limelight.

SEPTEMBER 1966: DAMAGE BY ROBBERS

The time was September 1966. In order to unite the opposition under a single candidate during the second term presidential elections, Pak Sunch'ŏn (the highest representative member of the People's Party) and non-ruling party politicians such as Yi In and Yi Pŏmsŏk, were pressuring Yun Posŏn (the candidate of the New Korea Party) to step down. They then dragged Yu Chino, the president of Korea University, into the political arena. While these events caught the attention of the political world, the newspapers' Society pages were running top stories on the investigation of a scandal involving Korea Fertilizer Company. Amid this chaotic atmosphere, the September 8 issue of all the newspapers ran a three-column article with photos under the headline 'Pulguksa Temple's Sŏkka Pagoda in Danger'. Information related to these events came out in a special report by the *JoongAng Ilbo* newspaper.

The Sŏkka Pagoda (National Treasure No. 21), which stands in front of Pulguksa Temple's Main Buddha Hall, was disturbed on the night of August 29 by light tremors (2 on the Richter Scale) in the

southern area of the East Sea. As a result, the pagoda is leaning about 6 degrees southward. Four stone pieces fell off the main body of the structure and the lower part of the base's cap stone cracked. This information was provided by a member of the Provincial Education Committee, who conducted an on-site survey of the site on the 8th.

Five days later, in the newspaper's September 13th issue, a six-column article appeared under the headline 'Divergent Explanations of the Sŏkka Pagoda's Destruction'.

Attention is now focused on the incident, as conclusions reached by the investigation team from the Committee of Cultural Properties Management concerning the cause of the Sŏkka Pagoda's destruction conflict with those of the local police and Pulguksa Temple. A team including Professor Hwang Suyŏng from the Committee of Cultural Properties Preservation and Im Pongshik from the Ministry of Education conducted a three-day, on-site inspection from the 9th to the 11th. Repudiating the previous assertion that the damage had been 'due to natural causes', they claimed that it was due to thieves trying to steal the pagoda's sarira reliquary and thus asked for a police investigation. On the morning of the 13th, the Office of Public Security received information that a thief had damaged Pulguksa Temple's Sŏkka Pagoda. It therefore dispatched Chŏng Sangch'ŏn, the office's chief of investigation, to lead an urgent inquiry.

On September 19, the police prosecutors finally announced that they had rounded up the thieves. On the following day, the newspaper printed a detailed analysis of the progress of the investigation and particulars of the crime under the title 'Circumstances Surrounding the National Treasure Thieves'.

On September 3, the thieves began by trying to lift the bottom level of the Sŏkka Pagoda, but were unable to do so as the jack was not strong enough. On the next day, they brought an air-jack with a 10-ton capacity from Taegu and lifted the pagoda's first story. During their third attempt on September 5, they lifted the second story and felt underneath with their hands but were unable to find the sarira.

The day after [they were captured], the thieves, in addition to the Sŏkka Pagoda theft, confessed to 13 felonies, all carried out within the last ten months. The Nawon Village Five-Story Pagoda has likewise been damaged by them, using a jack. Thirteen temples and ancient sites, including Hwangnyongsa Temple's foundation stones, the Namsansa Temple site and the T'ongdosa Temple Stele, have been ransacked by these thieves. The value of these historical treasures (5,500,000 won according to police estimates) is hard to fathom. At any rate, the police are prosecuting the nine members of the gang and are doing all they can to find the remaining ten accomplices and fences, in an attempt to recover the treasures.

At that time, the price of rice per *gama* (80 kilograms) was 4,300 won.

An inspection of the crime scene was subsequently carried out on September 23. The person who had received the stolen goods was Yi Pyŏnggak, President of Samgang Oils. Yi was arrested on charges of receiving stolen goods and for violation of the Cultural Properties Protection Law. The police confiscated a total of 226 cultural artifacts in his possession.

THE DAMAGE OF OCTOBER 1966

In order to restore the Sŏkka Pagoda to its original state, the Office of Cultural Properties formed a team of experts and began work on October 13. Then disaster struck again! On October 14, a front-page headline in the *JoongAng Ilbo* read, 'Tragedy Hits National Treasure Sŏkka Pagoda' above three photos showing the pagoda fracturing. Below the photos, the paper printed the following tragic report.

(Ch'oe Chongnyul, Yi Chongsŏk, Kim Yonggi and Ch'oe Kihwa reporting from Pulguksa Temple) Listed as National Treasure No. 21, the Sŏkka Pagoda (also known as the Muyŏng Pagoda) of Kyŏngju's Pulguksa Temple has suffered its greatest calamity. At two p.m. on the 13th, sighs of relief were heard when the pagoda's shiny gold sarira reliquary was discovered. Then just two hours later, the second-story roof-stone fell, breaking the third-story roof section. Already wounded by the hands of burglars, the pagoda has now sustained another wound during its restoration.

This was an exclusive report by the *JoongAng Ilbo*. According to the recollections of Ch'oe Chongnyul (former president of the *Kyunghyang Daily News*), there was at the time only one long-distance phone line at the Kyŏngju post office. A *JoongAng Ilbo* reporter got to it first, and was therefore able to send in the scoop as an exclusive. When viewed from the era of the cell phone, this is a charming aside. Papers at the time had only eight pages. The story's appearance on the top of page one shows the precedence given to this news. On the paper's 'Society' section, we find the following article lamenting the situation.

The old monks who saw today's accident at Pulguksa Temple were in tears, unable to control their deep grief. The dismantling of the pagoda was carried out by 11 people at 9:13 this morning. The on-site supervisor was Kim Ch'ŏnshŏk (52 years old), who is recognized as Korea's leading expert in Pagoda restoration. In his 32 years of experience, he has worked on around 25 pagodas of National Treasure caliber. The workmen were pushing things too far when they lowered the three-story roof stone and body in a single evening. The use of six bamboo poles fastened to an 8-meter-long telegraph pole [20 centimeters in diameter] as support was careless.

These days, this is simply unbelievable. The tools used for dismantling the Sŏkka Pagoda were a telegraph pole and bamboo shafts. The article continues:

The pulley barely managed to hoist the 7.5 ton, second-story roof-stone, but then broke, unable to bear the weight. At this point, the roof-stone had been lifted just 20 centimeters before it fell back. In spite of this, the construction team then tried a second time, but the telegraph pole, which was already bent, broke under the weight and the roof-stone, which was the size of a giant boulder, fell from its position in mid-air to the ground. It fell at an angle on the third-story roof-stone already on the ground, damaging it. Kim Ch'ŏnshŏk, beating his chest, said that he "had no idea that the inside of the telegraph pole was rotten."

The Sŏkka Pagoda mishap
While repairing the pagoda at 4 p.m. on October 13, 1966, workers dropped the second-story roof stone onto the body of the third-story, causing heavy damage. These three photos appeared on the front page of the JoongAng Ilbo.
1. Second-story roof stone being lifted.
2. The stone falls.
3. Broken roof stone.
(Courtesy of the JoongAng Ilbo).

As the roof-stone was being lowered, the Pulguksa Temple monks were chanting sutras with hands clasped in front of them. Amazingly, this scene was captured on film and printed in the day's newspaper. The reporter describes the monks' reactions as follows:

> The General Affairs Bureau of the Chogye Order had sent the monk Kang Sŏkch'ŏn as their representative to the site. Kang stamped his feet on the ground and cried out, "A shame for all ages!" He could not stop sobbing. Spectators at the scene became angry and tried to grab the workers but were stopped by the police.

The article also describes the frame of mind of the police and investigators as well as the measures they took after the disaster:

> The Kyŏngju Police Headquarters posted armed guards to keep a watch over the temple. Hwang Suyŏng, Chin Hongsŏp and Ch'oe Sunu from the Investigative Committee expressed deep regret over this damage to a national treasure, but were relieved that the harm had not been even greater. They said that restoration was still possible to some extent. However, the restoration of the second-story roof-stone probably will never be possible. This accident was a harsh wake-up call to the primitive and inane methods currently used to preserve cultural assets.

However, this 'wake-up call' was meaningless in the circumstances of the era. No special devices had been created for the repair and restoration of cultural assets; and the government, which was not interested in such matters, had likewise adopted no particular plan. At this time, even the head position at the Office of Cultural Properties was given to ex-military officers. Since even the thieves had managed to come up with a ten-ton jack, the level of the restoration project becomes immediately apparent. The news article ends on the following note:

> The restoration work recommenced with the cutting of five of the area's pine trees.

In other words, the only change in plans was to substitute fresh wood for the broken telegraph pole. Last autumn, I happened to mention this incident to my students. I thought that everyone was enjoying the story, but then one student, evidently still unable to understand, put forth an interesting question.

"Huh, that's strange. Aren't all telegraph poles made of concrete?"

New generation has evidently never seen a wooden pole!

A MAGNIFICENT TREASURE: THE SŎKKA PAGODA'S SARIRA RELIQUARY

The destruction of the Sŏkka Pagoda deserved to be the top story of the day. Yet we must not forget that the sarira container, found just two hours before the mishap, was a world-class cultural treasure and thus one of the greatest discoveries of the century. This find was also reported on the front page by the same reporters who had covered the other story.

As attention focused on the sarira reliquary after the attempted theft, the reliquary inside Pulguksa Temple's Sŏkka Pagoda was confirmed to be still intact. People gathered at the Shilla Cultural Festival when they learned of the discovery of the Sŏkka Pagoda's reliquary during the dismantlement of the pagoda. Indeed, the artifact is the essence of Shilla art and the highest realization of East Asian artistic thought. The crowd felt bitter-sweet emotions: the shock of the Sŏkka Pagoda's destruction was mixed with the joy of discovering a national treasure.

At 9 a.m. on the 13th, the pagoda's finial was dismantled under strict vigilance. At 2 p.m. as monks chanted sutras, the veil of mystery was removed from the second-story reliquary, which had lain hidden for well over a millennium.

This article gives the following detailed description of the reliquary's structure. I think that this is one of the best explanations of this elaborate artifact.

At the very center of the pagoda, there is a reliquary cavity 41 cm on all four sides and 18 cm deep. Here one finds a gilt-bronze sarira reliquary, covered with verdigris. It is surrounded by a miniature wooden pagoda, a bronze mirror, silk, fragrant cedar and gems, as well as a faint smell of incense from a millennium ago. The square, bronze outer-case (17 cm wide and 18 cm tall) has a magnificent symmetry like that of the Sŏkka Pagoda itself. Among sarira reliquaries found in Korea or around the world, this stands out as one of the greatest works of art.

The third sarira container was a 4 cm-tall vase covered with several layers of silk. Inside, there was a bean-sized, silver container wrapped in paper of pure gold. This rare item contained the actual sarira. In total, 48 sarira were found in the three containers mentioned above (46 from the sarira vase and one from each of the other containers).

In addition, there was a wooden printing block edition of the *Dharani Sutra* [in Korean, *Mugu chŏnggwang tae darani gyŏng*] wrapped in silk. 8 centimeters wide and 5 meters in length, the text was printed in clear Chinese characters on *hanji* [traditional Korean paper]. This valuable artifact attests to the high development of printing in Korea. Along with this, there was a lacquered item. It had

*THE SARIRA CONTAINERS FROM THE
SŎKKA PAGODA*
*Consisting of several containers
within each other, the sarira
reliquary inside the pagoda
included a glass jar, silver case
and gold box. Each of these can be
considered national treasures.*

deteriorated to the point that it was no longer possible to tell what it had been, but a high level of expertise was evident in the remnants of lacquer that were still clearly visible.

On the following day (October 15), pictures of the sarira containers were printed in the newspapers. The Chairman of the Committee of Cultural Properties, Dr. Kim Sanggi, and the director of the Office of Cultural Properties, Ha Kapch'ŏng, apologized to the public at an official news conference. News reports from the member of the Committee of Cultural Properties at the site said that they were optimistic that restoration of the pagoda would be possible. However, on the same newspaper page, there was extensive coverage of the conflict between the temple and the Committee of Cultural Properties concerning where the sarira should be housed.

How to preserve the sarira reliquary discovered in the Sŏkka Pagoda has now become an issue of conflict between the members of the Committee of Cultural Properties and the temple authorities. The latter are demanding that the sarira reliquary, which is now being housed in Kŭngnakchŏn (Paradise Hall), be returned to its original location within Sŏkka Pagoda. The Committee of Cultural Properties, concerned about chemical corrosion of the relics, say that they should be stored in a special manner.

The members of the Committee of Cultural Properties all agree that a special sarira preservation pavilion at least 66 meters wide should be built separately at the site, with special devices to prevent moisture and fire. The reliquary is presently being kept inside glass without any special measures. Everyone agrees that, if kept this way while waiting for a decision, important relics such as the silk and paper will deteriorate in less than a year.

It was later decided that special measures would be taken to preserve the sarira container. Meanwhile, Dr. Kim Sanggi, Kim Tujong and Kim Wonyong verified that the *Dharani Sutra* was the world's earliest extant text made with wooden printing blocks. Articles by the three scholars decorated ensuing issues of all the newspapers. After this, there was no more talk about the Sŏkka Pagoda's destruction and no mention of how the pagoda was to be restored.

At this point, the press writer Hong Chongin wrote what is probably his most famous editorial. Titled 'Who is Responsible for the Destruction of the Sŏkka Pagoda?' the article ran in the October 20 edition of the *JoongAng Ilbo*. This editorial was a harsh invective against those involved with the Sŏkka Pagoda's destruction. In particular, Hong criticized the irresponsible and insincere attitude of the people who had uttered remarks such as, "We're lucky that more damage wasn't done", "Korea's granite is so hard that we can just stick some metal bars in and put it back together", and "This was something I did with the faith of a Buddhist devotee." When something was wrong in the world, Hong was the kind of great journalist who could give people a severe dressing down.

There is probably no one who did not feel heart-rending pain and dread when they read the news reports about how the Sŏkka Pagoda at Pulguksa Temple in Kyŏngju broke into pieces.

Can this rash race of people, who boast of a 5000-year history, properly maintain the history and cultural heritage of this land? From somewhere, I can hear a scolding roll of thunder, ready to burst our eardrums.

A gang of thievs, greedy after treasure, ignoring the dignity of our national treasures, picks up the pagoda and rummages through it, causing partial damage. Even this brings on guilt that will not stop with the lives of the criminals. But then, in order to restore what the thieves have damaged, a group of people get involved under the name of the government, using government financing, whether it be large or small. Scholars and professors then get involved, calling in some workers to do the 'construction'. And these people break this pagoda, a national treasure, into pieces. Where is the honor we should feel in regard to this work passed down to us for well over a millennium? And when we think of the thousands of generations to come after us, what can we do to wash away this sin of rashness and negligence? Indeed, who is responsible for this? By all means, we must bring this to light.

I have heard that the work was given to so-and-so since he was trusted as someone familiar with this sort of thing. But what inspired such trust, and how was the person told to go about the work?

Some scholars do not want to differentiate the sequence of events clearly. It seems to me that they are putting excessive emphasis on the new national treasure, while taking the tragic destruction of the Sŏkka Pagoda, the mother of this national treasure, too lightly.

When we think of this in modern terms, isn't there a device called a 'crane' to be used in such constructions? Moreover, if the person is a specialist, when a part of a pagoda is lifted, he should be able to calculate the weight sufficiently according to the size of the stone. Who was trusted to do this work? In the end, we must conclude that the only thing trusted was rotten wood.

After Hong Chong'in's editorial, nothing else appeared in the papers about the Sŏkka Pagoda. Nobody is aware that another very important and tragic event occurred at Pulguksa Temple around this time. Even

now, almost no one knows about this. A green vase containing 46 sarira had been the highlight among the sarira implements found in the Sŏkka Pagoda. However, a monk, when moving the vase, dropped it. The priceless relic shattered into pieces. The pieces were glued back together, and it now sits in the storage room at the National Museum. In the Pulguksa Temple Restoration Report, there is the following explanation, accompanied by a black and white photo before the accident.

Made of dark green glass, the sarira vase (6.45 cm high, mouth: 1.5 cm in diameter, body: 5 cm in diameter, neck: 1.8 cm in diameter) is the largest item. There are 46 sarira inside the vase. Above the round body, which is nearly circular, there is a short neck with a lip. The semitransparent surface is speckled here and there and the bottom is slightly concave. This sarira reliquary was on display with other religious implements in Pulguksa Temple's Paradise Hall, but, due to the carelessness of a monk, was damaged and can therefore no longer be seen in its complete form.

This was a disaster on par with that of the Sŏkka Pagoda.

RESTORATION PROCESS DURING THE 1970S

In the late spring of 1969, the political world focused on whether Park Chung-hee would change the Constitution to allow himself a third term. On May 12, President Park ordered the restoration of Pulguksa Temple. The project took four years and resulted in the Pulguksa Temple we know today. It was an extensive undertaking requiring an enormous budget. In the *Pulguksa Temple Restoration Report*, there is a detailed schedule listing 40 steps. Looking at these, one can get a sense of Park's strong determination to restore cultural assets. In Korea's economic situation, funds were difficult to procure, but the project was pushed through and completed by the strong government of the time. Below is a summary of the key steps in the project.

1. May 12, 1969   Park orders restoration.
2. May 21, 1969   Minister of Culture and Information [the former Ministry of Education] meets with top businessman and management in order to garner support for the main project.
4. June 17, 1969   At the Financial Affairs Secretariat of the Blue House, the restoration of Pulguksa Temple as well as repair of and clean-up work on Haengju Mountain Fortress, Tosan Sŏwon [Confucian academy] and Chinju Fortress is discussed.
5. June 23, 1969   At Korea House in Seoul, management, research and design committees are formed as a part of the Pulguksa Temple Restoration Committee.
8. July 30, 1969   At Sejong Hotel, there is a meeting with donors in order to collect funds for the project.
13. August 29 to October 30, 1969   Excavation of Pulguksa Temple.
18. November 14, 1969   Commencement ceremony for the restoration of Pulguksa Temple

35. February 6, 1972   His Excellency the President Park tours Pulguksa Temple, gives advice on applying the bright and dim paint on the eaves, tells workers to do their jobs with utmost sincerity, and praises the efforts of the respective ministries.

36. June 18, 1972   His Excellency the President comes to the temple and advises the workers to use slightly more subdued shades of paint on the eaves.

39. July 3, 1973   His Excellency the President is invited for the Pulguksa Temple Restoration Completion Ceremony.

Pulguksa Temple's Forgotten Beauty

Pulguksa Temple was thus restored. As a result, I am at least able to point it out as Korea's greatest piece of architecture, and for this, I am thankful to all those who worked on the project. We have developed in so many ways since then. We have come a long way in terms of technological capability, research methods and outlook. And these changes are, in the end, part of our cultural and historical progress. For this reason, I must also look at the restoration from a more modern standpoint and discuss the beauty that has been lost.

The first mistake was the failure to reconstruct the Kyŏngnu (Sutra Pavilion). As mentioned previously, Pulguksa Temple had a completely symmetrical design. Standing in the courtyard in front of the Main Buddha Hall, one can't help but feel a lack of balance when looking at the elaborate Tabo Pagoda and simple Sŏkka Pagoda. This is the same whether seen from the perspective of the Buddha image or from Chahamun (Purple Mist Gate). This lack of balance was originally offset by Kyŏngnu and Chongnu (Belfry). At present, instead of the former, one sees only the 'Four Articles' (drum, bell, gong and wooden fish). Originally, there was a simple, closed-off building here. The belfry, also known as Pŏmyŏngnu (Floating Reflection Pavilion), is an elaborate structure. For this reason, it is also known as 'Mt. Sumeru Belfry' (Sumi

Pŏmjonggak). Thus, from the perspective of the Buddha image, beyond the elaborate Tabo Pagoda on the left stood the simple Kyŏngnu. And beyond the simple Sŏkka Pagoda on the right, stood the ornate Chongnu. In other words, opposites were symmetrically opposed and thus formed a unity. According to the temple's basic plan, this had to be the case.

Second, when the Sŏkka Pagoda was restored, the added finial was too ornate. Since no one knew what the original finial had looked like, the finial from the Shilsangsa Temple Pagoda in Namwon was replicated. The Shilsang Pagoda, though modeled after the Sŏkka Pagoda, was a comparatively elegant and ornate pagoda from the ninth century. If the builders wanted to use such a finial on the Sŏkka Pagoda, they should have made it less elaborate, in keeping with the simple and elegant beauty of the structure. If the decorative protuberances were simply removed from the present finial, it would agree with the general atmosphere of the pagoda.

Third, Kŭngnakchŏn (Paradise Hall) is dilapidated. The hall was rebuilt in 1750 after it burned down during the Hideyoshi Invasions (1592-1598). At this time, instead of using pillars that had been cut straight, warped timber was used. These twisting pillars do not fit in well with the solemn look of the foundation. Such twisted timber would look nice on a mountain temple, especially if it sat on a natural stone embankment that was joined with the foundation using the *kŭraeng'i* technique. However, it simply looks affected and shabby next to Pulguksa Temple's galleries and geometric architecture.

The fourth fault is perhaps the worst: the failure to restore the Kup'um Yŏnji (Nine Grades Lotus Pond) during the 1970 restoration. According the *Pulguksa Temple Restoration Report*, at the ninth meeting of the Pulguksa Temple Restoration Research Committee, the group decided against restoring the pond, which was being excavated at the time. The decision was based on concerns that the trees and remaining structures

A COMPARISON OF THE SHILSANGSA TEMPLE AND SŎKKA PAGODAS
When restored, the Sŏkka Pagoda was given a finial modeled
after the one on the Shilsangsa Temple Pagoda.
However, the finial from the ornate Shilsangsa Temple
Pagoda does not go well with the elegant and somewhat
austere Sŏkka Pagoda.

might be disturbed along with visitor facilities. This may have been the case, but by neglecting to rebuild the pond, the temple's stonework retains only a fraction of its former beauty.

The Kup'um Yŏnji was an oval lotus pond situated below the Blue Cloud and White Cloud Bridges. It measured 39.5 m from east to west and 25.5 m from north to south. The pond's perimeter was made up of the same large, uncut stones used in the temple's stonework. The pond was 2 to 3 meters deep, and the water is believed to have come down from the Mt. T'ohamsan Valley through an underground aqueduct that ran along the gallery to the east of the Main Buddha Hall. It then ran through a stone channel next to the Blue Cloud Bridge before falling into the pond. Water is also thought to have come from the spring below Kyŏngnu (which is the spring still in use). In Kup'um Yŏnji which was always brimming with clear water, one could see the inverted reflection of Pŏmyŏngnu along with the temple's elaborate stonework. Indeed, this is how Pŏmyŏngnu (Floating Reflection Pavilion) got its name.

When I visit Pulguksa Temple, I invariably go in the early morning when there are few people. During the summer, fall and spring, one can sense the moisture in the atmosphere as a light mist hovers in the cool morning air. When the pond existed, the Blue Cloud and White Cloud Bridges would naturally have been shrouded in fog every morning. At this time, Chahamun would have really looked like a 'Purple Mist Gate', and Pulguk (Buddha Land)-sa Temple would have truly seemed like the architectural realization of the realm of the Buddha. Unable to actually see such a sight, I close this section with feelings of regret and sorrow.

Namu Pulguksa Temple, Namu Pulguksa Temple

While writing this book, I have combed through many old texts, trying to find poems appropriate for each historical site. Although I was sometimes unable to find anything suitable, I've usually come up with something. I also looked for poetry about Pulguksa Temple. I finally came across the *Poetry Collection of Ancient Sites in Kyŏngju*.[5] This work, mimeographed by the Archaeology and Art Association, contained works by great poets such as Ch'oe Ch'iwon, Kim Shisŭp, Kim Chongjik and Yi Ŏnjŏk. Yet when I read over the poems of Kim Chŏng-hŭi, Master Choŭi and Pak Mogwol, I couldn't find anything appropriate. It wasn't because I didn't feel these were great poems. Rather, it was because these poets' descriptions were so subjective. The poems were filled with poetic exclamations such as, "Ah, I've grown old! Ah, time is transient!" and "Alas, it has become a ruin." Many of the poems could have been discussing any old monastery—there was no reason why it had to be Pulguksa Temple. Nothing could be more surprising and disappointing. Architecture may be silent, but how could these insensitive poets, our indifferent ancestors, have been silent for a thousand years in front of this majestic stonework and these picturesque pagodas?

For this grand temple, which all these grand poets failed to praise, there is nothing else to do. I must take up my pen and praise it, in the style of the ancient poets, with my awkward verse. The title of this piece is 'Namu Pulguksa Temple'.

Where the sun rises in Sŏrabŏl lies the sacred mountain East Peak.

Emitting (*t'o*) sunshine and gathering (*ham*) moonlight, it is known as Mt. T'ohamsan.

Sacred halls of antiquity have been built on the side of Mt. T'ohamsan.

King Kyŏngdŏk brought everything under Heaven to fruition, yet lacked a successor.

Was this a divine test, to create an artistic monarch?

Grand Master P'yohun rushes to meet the celestial deity;

A mountain's cut, earth's moved and a Buddha land is formed.

Large boulders, stones from a brook and straight stone blocks are placed in a stone embankment.

"Let us give alms, Let us give alms."

Namu Pulguksa Temple

Across Kup'um Yŏnji,

Lie the White Cloud and Blue Cloud Bridges,

Over these cloud-bridges, Chahamun,

Over the Seven Gems Bridge and the Lotus Flower Bridge,

Lies Anyangmun.

There, one finds Mt. Sumeru.

There, one finds paradise.

In front of the large Buddha in the Main Buddha Hall,

Stand sacred pagodas to the sides of a bright stone lamp.

Surrounded by long galleries, there is only moonlight and starlight.

All songs can be heard in the rustling of Mt. T'ohamsan's pines.

"Magnificent. Magnificent. Truly magnificent."

Namu Pulguksa Temple

A jeweled pagoda stands tall

In accordance with the Tabo Buddha's vow.

Amitabha became a great Buddha after making 48 vows.

How is it that Kim Taesŏng never saw the Buddha land?

How did Asadal lose his mistress, Asanyŏ?

The East Peak slope is so steep: there's no time for a cigarette.

The pagoda's reflection never appears at sunset in the reflecting pond.

As summer and autumn pass,

Foreign enemies gather across mountain and sea,

The 3,000 k'an[6] of Pulguksa Temple go up in a big fire.

"What shall we do? What shall we do? What shall we do with this great sorrow?"

Namu Pulguksa Temple

The temple monks depart, leaving an empty site.

Yet the rocks of Shilla are so grand.

Though one in ten remains, it's magnificent.

The Japanese come again and take away some stone lions,

A roof stone held with a telegraph pole falls and cracks.

A bluish sarira bottle shatters.

Filled with earth, Kup'um Yŏnji has flowers no more.

The round moon floats high o'er Mt. T'ohamsan's slope

White moonlight and a clear breeze mix and turn moist.

Sakyamuni, Tabo Buddha, Great King Kyŏngdŏk,

Grand Master P'yohun, Kim Taesŏng, Asadal— the ancient masters of this temple watch over the temple.

Sighing, Heaven's words can be heard in the wind and birdsong,

"What did you trust? What did you trust?"

Namu Pulguksa Temple

Namu Pulguksa Temple

Namu Pulguksa Temple[7]

June 1997

1. "Tonggyŏng kihaeng".
2. Translation of original Japanese title.
3. *Han'guk munhwajae sunansa* (Seoul: Tolbegae, 1996).
4. Translation of original Japanese title.
5. *Kyŏngju kojŏk shimunjip.*
6. A unit of measurement.
7. "Namu" is used here to mean "take refuge in". However, the author has altered the Chinese characters of the last "namu" to mean "How can it be absent?"

PART 2

Stroll through Sŏrabŏl

Smiles of the Baby Buddha

Ch'ŏmsŏngdae / Nine-Story Pagoda of Hwangnyongsa Temple /
Samhwaryŏng Maitreya Triad / Stone Niche Buddha / Yŏgŭn Valley

SEAT NUMBER 33 ON THE EXPRESS BUS

Previously, on those rare occasions when I had a chance to travel on my own, I preferred to take the bus instead of the train. Although the train was undoubtedly much more comfortable, it meant being tied down by time-tables, not to mention extra expense and, worst of all, it had a distracting atmosphere. Sitting on the train, there was always the chance that I'd end up next to a pair of prattling girls or a whining child. Of course, the same thing could happen while riding the bus, but since people tend to doze off after a few minutes, the hubbub would never last long.

When buying my bus ticket, I always asked for seat numbers 25 or 33. These two window-seats were behind the driver in the middle of the bus, and the wide windows weren't blocked by partitions. Since the seat numbers were past 20, they were in the smoking section and were back far enough to avoid the noise if a video was played. Although I occasionally took the right hand seats numbers 28 or 36 in order to avoid the sun, I usually stuck to seat number 33. And when I was in my favorite seat, I was usually on the way to one of my favorite destinations: Kyŏngju.

105

*The object of continuous debate among scholars of the history of Korean science,
Ch'ŏmsŏngdae's elegant shape resembles the Shilla pottery pieces known as kidae.*

CH'ŎMSŎNGDAE: A GREAT CAUSE FOR DISAPPOINTMENT

It takes at least a month to properly appreciate Kyŏngju. During the
typical two or three-day tour, it's impossible to see, let alone understand,
the area's numerous historical sites.

Korean textbooks rightfully describe the area as a repository of Korea's
brilliant cultural heritage. As students, Koreans hear time after time
glowing praise of both Kyŏngju and the Shilla monuments found there.
For our history, language and art exams, we have to memorize countless
facts about the area. Many of us have even visited the city on school field
trips. Yet for precisely this reason, Kyŏngju is often a major

disappointment. Although we hear praises of the city so often, we have seldom had an opportunity to actually learn what is behind such extravagant acclamations.

For those who travel to Kyŏngju for the first time full of expectation, one of the biggest letdowns is Chŏmsŏngdae. The structure, which our school textbooks describe as the first observatory in Northeast Asia, does not even reach 10 meters in height. By "observatory" do the textbooks mean to tell us that people used to crawl up to the top? Are we supposed to believe that the heavens look any closer from that height? If so, why wasn't it built on a moutain, or at the very least, on the nearby hill at Panwolsŏng (Half-Moon Fortress). If anything, the structure would seem to represent a tremendous poverty and dullness in the Shilla people's imagination.

However, the poverty and dullness are not to be attributed to the Shilla people, but rather lie with the educators of the present day who have mistakenly dubbed the structure Northeast Asia's first observatory. The average person has never had the opportunity to properly learn about Chŏmsŏngdae's fascinating structure and symbolism.

THE SYMBOLISM HIDDEN IN CHŎMSŎNGDAE'S STRUCTURE

Chŏmsŏngdae is situated in modern Kyŏngju's Inwang-dong, but in Shilla times the site would have been just above Panwolsŏng (the site of the royal palace) and Kyerim (Chicken Forest), not far from Tumuli Park, Sŏkpinggo (Stone Ice Cellar) and Anapchi (Goose and Duck Pond). In other words, it wasn't located in the downtown section of the ancient Shilla capital, but in the area of government buildings. Shilla's national meteorological and astronomical observatories were situated in the same area.

During Shilla times, the national meteorological observatory would have included other buildings. As with other wooden structures from the Shilla period, these buildings are no longer extant. All that remains at the site is Chŏmsŏngdae, which served as the structure symbolizing the functions of the observatories.

Chŏmsŏngdae's enigmatic stone structure has given rise to a heated debate about the functions of it among those who study the history of Korean science, and scholars are still unable to reach an agreement. Among the ideas which have been set forth, I find the following particularly persuasive.

Let us first imagine that we were to establish a structure to represent astronomical observation in the National Meteorological Observatory at Sŏdaemun in modern Seoul. What type of building would we construct? The designers would probably attempt to create a symbol of modern-day astronomical knowledge. Likewise, it is believed that the Shilla people created Chŏmsŏngdae as a structure symbolizing the level of astronomical knowledge which they had attained.

Chŏmsŏngdae's general shape resembles a stand. Many science historians have described it as a bottle shape, but more likely, the shape represents the stands used to support ritual vessels. Indeed, many stands with a similar shape have been discovered among Shilla pottery. For this reason, the structure is called Chŏmsŏngdae (literally, Observing Stars Platform) instead of Chŏmsŏngt'ap (Observing Stars Stupa)or Chŏmsŏng'ok (Observing Stars Building). The syllable *dae* (platform) is not meant to suggest that people climbed on top, but rather that the structure was a platform supporting Heaven. In Northeast Asia, tradition has it that Heaven is round and Earth is square. For this reason, Chŏmsŏngdae's base is square while the body is round. Professor Park Sŏngnae describes Chŏmsŏngdae as follows on page 433 of his work *Special Lectures on Korean History.*[1]

The body of the structure is made up of 27 layers of stones. If the top stonework, which is shaped like a tic-tac-toe board, is included, it brings the number to 28. These layers are thought to symbolize the basic constellations which in Northeast Asia number 28. If the base is included, there are 29 layers—the number of days in a lunar month. On the structure's southern face, there is a window with 12 layers of stones above and below it. Taken separately, these are thought to represent the 12 months of the year, and when taken together, the 24 seasonal divisions. The number of stones making up the body of the structure differs slightly depending on where one begins one's count, but comes to approximately 362—roughly the days in a solar year.

Ch'ŏmsŏngdae also functioned as a device for precisely determining the movements of the sun. As described on page 54 of Professor Chŏn Sang-un's work *History of Korean Science and Technology*.[2]

> The four sides of the structure's square base face north, east, south and west, while the top piece is offset so that it faces the intermediate directions (northeast, northwest, southeast and southwest). The window faces directly south. As a result, when the sun is situated directly to the south during the autumnal and vernal equinoxes, the sun's rays pass through the window lighting up the entire floor of the structure. During the summer and winter solstices, on the other hand, the floor becomes completely dark. In this way, Ch'ŏmsŏngdae was used to gauge the mid-point and terminus of the four seasons.

What exquisite design and amazing symbolism! Even when its scientific practicality is disregarded, Ch'ŏmsŏngdae is striking simply for its grace and elegance. The upper square piece is exactly half the size of the base, giving the structure a feeling of stability, while its body gently curves inward with a sense of elegance and warmth characteristic of Shilla art.

According to tradition, Ch'ŏmsŏngdae was constructed during the reign of Queen Sŏndŏk (r. 632-646). For this reason, some scholars have suggested that the structure's 27 layers of stone blocks represent the queen's position as the kingdom's 27th ruler; yet the correspondence is most likely coincidental. What is certain, however, is that Chŏmsŏngdae is one of the invaluable artifacts made in the reign of Queen Sŏndŏk which give vivid testimony to Shilla's one thousand-year-old culture.

Three Artifacts that Offer a Glimpse of Shilla's Glory

The best way to improve our appreciation of cultural artifacts is to view important relics with a knowledgeable teacher. I was fortunate enough to learn about Kyŏngju from the respected authority Chŏng Yangmo, who is also known under the pen-name Sobul (Laughing Buddha). Sobul presently heads the Cultural Research Department of the National Museum (in March 1993, he was promoted to chief curator), but he previously served two terms as the chief curator of Kyŏngju National Museum. I visited him often when he was there to join him on historical surveys or to get his help, and occasionally to give him some help with his work. The following episode occurred on a summer day in 1985 when I dropped by to see Sobul while passing through the area.

We had just finished dinner and had returned to his residence, and then he turned to me and said, "Tell me, in order, what are your favorite sites in Kyŏngju?"

"I suppose they'd be Sŏkkuram, the Sŏkka, Kosŏnsa Temple and Kamŭnsa Temple Pagodas, the Baby Buddhas of Samhwaryŏng, the turtle-shaped stele base at King Muyŏl's Tomb, the fairy depictions on the Emille Bell,[3] the rock carving of Buddha at the Yongjangsa Temple site on Mt. Namsan, the niche-carving of Buddha at Pulgok, rock carving of Buddha at the Samnŭng Valley, and the Medicine Buddha statue at Porisa Temple...something like that." These sites would later be discussed in my books since they were, and have remained, my favorites. I'm sure most people's choice of key sites would be similar.

Sobul, after a long pause, asked me, "Have you ever been to King

Chinp'yŏng's Tomb?"

"No."

"How about the Changhangsa Temple site?"

"No."

"Have you personally heard the sound of the Emille Bell being struck?"

"No."

"To be able to say anything about Kyŏngju, one must have experienced these three things, for they give a sense of the ancient city's character."

Sobul said no more about the matter. With my confidence somewhat shaken, I could not bring myself to ask him what he meant. Instead, I promised to return, sure that I would understand after a visit to the sites he mentioned.

When I did so, I had to agree that the sound of the Emille Bell was magnificent. And the Changhangsa Temple site was truly impressive. However, I simply could not see what was so magnificent or impressive about King Chinp'yŏng's Tomb.

After that first visit, I probably returned to the tomb on ten different occasions. On each visit to Kyŏngju, it would always be the first stop on my itinerary. Nevertheless, Sobul's claim that it was one of the three Kyŏngju sites that must be seen remained for me a most puzzling riddle. I felt like a Zen monk hopelessly struggling to comprehend some enigmatic phrase of the master. In my attempt to get to the bottom of the matter, I visited the site at different times, going in the dead of night, on a spring day when the wild flowers were in bloom and in the winter when the ground was carpeted with snow. Although I knew it was forbidden, I even climbed on top. In spite of all these preparations for some great epiphany, nothing much happened. During this time, I led five or six tours of Kyŏngju but always skipped the tomb as I didn't feel up to discussing it.

The riddle constantly dogged me during my subsequent trips to

Kyŏngju. Sobul's authoritative knowledge of the area was indisputable, so I was unable merely to drop the matter and conclude that he had been mistaken. I even brought Sobul with me on three occasions hoping to get at least some hint of what lay behind his statement, but he would merely say, "Feel the atmosphere of this place. It's really good." And each time, I despondently agreed out of courtesy.

Finally seven years later during the spring of this year, as I sat in seat number 33 and watched the full moon trail behind our bus, I suddenly understood what Sobul had meant about the good atmosphere. The three sites which he had mentioned weren't important as visible art relics. However, they did give one a sense of the setting in which Shilla's brilliant culture was created. Each relic reflected a particular aspect of Shilla culture, with King Chinp'yŏng's Tomb attesting to Shilla culture during the early seventh century, the Changhangsa Temple site an indication of the culture during the late seventh century and the Emille Bell representing that of the mid-eighth century.

GENTLE YET FIRM: KING CHINP'YŎNG'S TOMB

King Chinp'yŏng's Tomb is situated next to a rice paddy in Kuhwang-dong at the eastern foot of Mt. Nangsan. To get to the tomb from downtown Kyŏngju, one passes by Punhwangsa Temple as if going to the Pomun Tourist Resort Complex. After going through a rotary, one takes the first right onto a farm road. Across the planted fields, there is a line of trees which leads up to the tomb. According to Sobul, the proper way to see the tomb is to walk past these old trees. Unfortunately, some trees from the middle of the line were felled in order to make an irrigation canal. Sobul always regretted this damage to the tomb's picturesque entrance.

The tomb consists of a large mound rising up at the end of the arbored path. It is surrounded by large, stately pines with twisted trunks, reminiscent of landscapes by the famous Ming writer and painter Wen

KING CHINP'YŎNG'S TOMB   In the calm, royal atmosphere of this tomb, one can sense the vigor that enabled Shilla to unite the Three Kingdoms.

Zhengming (1470-1559). From my experience, the tomb area is most beautiful during May or June when the wild crysanthemums are in full bloom.

There are no decorations on the mound except for 12 large, uncut stones along the tomb's edge. Corresponding to the points on a compass, the stones have been set within the earth in a subdued fashion with one surface barely exposed. They form a striking contrast with the 12 zodiacal figures of Kim Yushin's Tomb or the elaborately sculpted figures next to Koerŭng (Suspended Tomb). In these later tombs, we see the tendency towards embellishment that developed in the Unified Shilla period. On the other hand, King Chinp'yŏng's Tomb also lacks the awesome grandeur of the earlier Chŏnmach'ong (Heavenly Horse Tomb). Yet of the 155 ancient tombs of Kyŏngju, King Chinp'yŏng's Tomb is the only one that combines a sense of royal dignity with a gentle, subdued air.

The only other tomb that may be said to possess these qualities is that of Queen Sŏndŏk (King Chinp'yŏng's daughter) situated on the peak of Mt. Nangsan. If one is only able to appreciate extravagant and decorative art, the refined qualities of King Chinp'yŏng's Tomb are likely to go unnoticed. Indeed, works like this tomb can never appear in a capricious cultural and social milieu in which people are only satisfied with elaborate embellishments.

WHAT DO YOU KNOW ABOUT QUEEN SŎNDŎK?

Who built King Chinp'yŏng's Tomb? It was constructed by his daughter, Queen Sŏndŏk, a key figure from Korea's past.

Textbooks on the nation's history, when describing the development and flowering of Shilla culture, generally begin with King Pŏphŭng (r. 514-539) since this king, by adopting Buddhism, provided Shilla with a firm philosophical foundation. Textbooks typically go on to describe the key events in Shilla's bid to unify the Three Kingdoms, using tales of Kim Yushin and King Muyŏl (r. 654-660). Students cannot be blamed for concluding that the interim reigns of King Chinp'yŏng and Queen Sŏndŏk, marred by the war between the Three Kingdoms, were periods of cultural stagnation.

Yet when we look at the cultural artifacts from the period before Shilla's unification of the Three Kingdoms, we find that they were nearly all created during the reigns of King Chinp'yŏng and Queen Sŏndŏk. The famous gilt-bronze Maitreya figure with one foot resting on the other knee (National Treasure No. 83) as well as the Buddha triad on Mt. Namsan's Sŏnbanggok (Meditation Hall Valley) are believed to date from the reign of King Chinp'yŏng, while relics from the reign of Queen Sŏndŏk include the nine-story pagoda of Hwangnyongsa Temple, Punhwangsa Temple, Ch'ŏmsŏngdae, the Samhwaryŏng Baby Buddhas and the niche-carving of Buddha in Pulgok (Buddha Valley) on Mt. Namsan. In short, if we exclude royal tombs, virtually all of the major relics that are extant date from this period.

These two reigns also produced many of Korea's leading historical figures, such as Dharma Master Won'gwang (King Chinp'yŏng's reign) and Vinaya Master Chajang (Queen Sŏndŏk's reign). The famous monks Wonhyo and Ŭisang also spent their formative years under the reign of Queen Sŏndŏk. Why, then, do history books often fail to even mention King Chinp'yŏng while describing Queen Sŏndŏk, in terms reminiscent of the unofficial histories, as a somewhat brazen-faced ruler? It may be that they are uncritically following the evaluation of Kim Pushik, the author of *Historical Records of the Three Kingdoms.*[4] Kim, who evidently held some rather 'unprogressive' ideas about women, concludes his section on Queen Sŏndŏk by saying, "China may have had empresses, but a woman was never made emperor. Appointing a woman king in opposition to the principles of *yin* and *yang*,[5] was truly an action forced by turbulent times. The country was fortunate to avoid ruin." Kim ridicules the queen as "a weak pig dancing around," with the implication that during a woman's reign, the kingdom's culture cannot but decline. Reading between the lines, we can sense how brilliantly culture blossomed during the period.

Queen Sŏndŏk's talent, sensibility and magnanimity are evident in the accounts of her three prophecies. Her magnanimity is also evident when we look at the massive nine-story pagoda that once stood in the Hwangnyongsa (Imperial Dragon) Temple.

THE GRANDEUR OF HWANGNYONGSA TEMPLE'S NINE-STORY PAGODA

To the south of Punhwangsa Temple, one finds the site of Hwangnyongsa Temple. For years now, an extensive archeological excavation has been underway at the site. In ancient times, a nine-story wooden pagoda stood here, the size of which can be surmised by the foundation stones which have been discovered. One side of the pagoda's square base measured 22.2 meters, making the ground area covered by the pagoda 495.87 square meters! According to the *Memorabilia of the Three Kingdoms,*[6] the nine-story wooden pagoda's finial (top portion) measured 42 *chŏk* (similar to feet) while its main body measured 183 *ch'ŏk*; hence, its full height would have been 225 *ch'ŏk* (about 68 meters). Looked at in terms of modern architecture, it would have been equal to a 20-story building with a transmission tower on top. When Korean art students hear this during a lecture, they glance skeptically at their professor, but their disbelief turns to astonishment when they personally visit the excavation site. Looking at the actual site, one realizes the tremendous scale of Queen Sŏndŏk's projects.

Apart from size, there are two other aspects of the temple site that amaze me. Construction of this temple, which eventually covered close to 100,000 square meters, began in 553 during the 14th year of King Chinhŭng's reign. It took 17 years to complete the construction project which was finalized with the building of the walls, while the main Buddha figure wasn't completed until 21 years later (574) and the Main Buddha Hall 31 years later (584). As for the nine-story wooden pagoda, it wasn't finished until 645, or 92 years after the commencement of the project. In other words, it took nearly a century to complete the construction of the temple. Damaged by lightning in 698, the temple underwent restoration in 720. Several decades later in 754, the temple bell, three times larger than the famous Emille Bell, was finally completed. If we consider the bell as the final element of the temple's basic layout, the monastery took two centuries to build.

Generations of builders had to work on this project with unflagging care and determination. How are we to understand their dedication? Hwangnyongsa Temple gives us cause to reflect on the current era, when both individuals and nations only undertake a project based on the premise that it must yield immediate benefits. In the current era, who would plant a fruit tree that could only bear fruit after 90 years?

The second aspect of the temple I find surprising is that Shilla

EXCAVATION OF THE HWANGNYONGSA TEMPLE SITE This photo, taken from the air, gives one a sense of the ancient temple's massive size. The grove of trees at the top surrounds the Punhwangsa Temple site.

requested the Paekche government to send Abiji, a master architect of the Paekche Kingdom, to help design the temple's nine-story pagoda. Perhaps what is even more amazing is that historians accept this with almost total indifference! If, as historians all assure us, this period was one of continual warfare among the Three Kingdoms, how could two feuding nations make or grant such a request? Moreover, records state that the pagoda's nine stories were to provide spiritual protection against invasion by nine enemy states. The list of unfriendly states includes China and Japan as well as the Malgal and Yemaek peoples but fails to include both Koguryŏ and Paekche!

This brings up a question: Were the battles during Queen Sŏndŏk's reign undertaken in an attempt to subjugate the neighboring kingdoms so as to unify the peninsula, or were they ongoing skirmishes that had always taken place? At what point did these tit-for-tat clashes turn into an all-out war for unification? Any conclusive answer to this question must take into account cultural history. In particular, we cannot overlook the extensive influence that Paekche had on Shilla culture during the reigns of King Chinp'yŏng and Queen Sŏndŏk. Thanks to this influence and stimulus, Shilla systematically acquired and developed its own ancient culture. From Paekche's standpoint, it was exporting the advanced culture that had developed around the time of King Mu (r. 600-641).

Ch'ŏmsŏngdae's elegant yet gentle contours are actually more typical of Paekche art than that of Shilla. During these years of cultural development, the Shilla people had been inspired by Paekche art. They eventually assimilated it and made it their own, creating the vital culture of Shilla's heyday. Due to this cultural borrowing, the artifacts from Queen Sŏndŏk's reign have a warm, gentle, human quality that isn't found in the art of preceding or later periods. When Sobul referred to the atmosphere of King Chinp'yŏng's Tomb, he was referring to this quality.

THE BABY BUDDHAS OF SAMHWARYŎNG

Among the cultural relics from Queen Sŏndŏk's reign, the Samhwaryŏng Baby Buddhas are the most charming. Officially known as the Saeng'ŭisa Temple Maitreya Triad, its three figures were originally situated on Samhwaryŏng Hill on Mt. Namsan. The *in situ* central figure was placed in the Kyŏngju Museum in 1925, whereas the two attendant Bodhisattva figures, which had been stolen by a local resident, were confiscated and reunited with the central figure at the museum, where they are currently displayed.

Doctor Hwang Suyŏng is credited with pointing out that these figures were the Saeng'ŭisa Temple Maitreya Triad mentioned in the *Memorabilia of the Three Kingdoms*. This classical historical work tells us that the statues were carved in 644, the 13th year of Queen Sŏndŏk's reign.

The body proportions of these charming figures correspond to those of a child. With an innocent smile and lovable countenance, the carvings

Saengŭisa Temple Maitreya Triad Originally situated on Samhwaryŏng Hill on Kyŏngju's Mt. Namsan, the triad is now on display at the Kyŏngju National Museum.

are totally captivating. In particular, the left-hand Bodhisattva, in spite of its broken nose, exquisitely expresses the melding of the enlightened mind of Buddha with the innocent mind of a child. Although it is impossible to know when the practice started, visitors to Samhwaryŏng Hill clearly used to rub their hands over the childlike faces and hands of these figures, which came to be known as the Samhwaryŏng Baby Buddhas.

In 1979, at the end of Park Chung-hee's era of 'Revitalizing Reform's', "Five Thousand Years of Korean Art" was planned as a three-year exhibition which would tour seven major cities in the United States. This ambitious endeavor was supposedly undertaken in order to promote a positive image of Korean culture. It was actually nothing more than a diversionary tactic. Park used the shield of culture to block the arrows of criticism over his dictatorship's appalling human rights record. At any rate, these Baby Buddhas with their childlike faces were some of the items selected. In preparation for their international debut, the Baby Buddhas were given their first bath. The curators of the museum had to soak the carvings in laundry detergent for three days in order to wash off

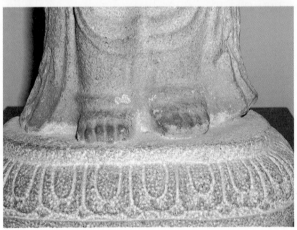

*THE CHARMING COUNTENANCE OF
ONE OF THE 'BABY BUDDHAS'*
A childlike innocence is
combined with the Buddha-
mind in this figure's lovely
face and tranquil smile.

BABY BUDDHAS' TOES
The grimy hands of
mischievous children have
blackened the toes of
these Buddhas.

a millennium of encrusted grime. This may explain why the earlier and later photos of the sculptures look so different.

THE BABY BUDDHAS' BLACK TOES

After three years of traveling, the Baby Buddhas were reunited with their relatives in the Buddhist statue exhibit at the Kyŏngju Museum. However, it was soon discovered that their toes had turned pitch black. Perplexed, I went to Sobul and asked about this. In his typically enigmatic fashion, he responded, "If you stand for a few hours in front of the images, you'll figure it out yourself." Following his instructions, I stood aimlessly in front of the statues and sure enough, in less than an hour the answer came to me. (If only the riddle of King Chinp'yŏng's Tomb had been so easy!)

Kyŏngju Museum averages more than 20,000 visitors each day. From morning to evening, crowds of school kids of all ages, foreign and domestic tour groups and honeymooners push past the exhibits. At times, people even have to stand in line outside each hall. Of course, the high school students eventually manage to slip away from the 'boring old relics' and run around outside, but the elementary and middle school students, still wary of the teacher's sharp glances, are forced to march through each room. Looking at the students' blank expressions, it is clear that they are not moved by what they see. They absentmindedly pass by a piece of stone that was a prehistoric ax or a sooty earthenware bowl. Their faces briefly light up as they glance at the gold crowns and earrings but their eyes glaze over again as they pass the inexplicably large display of broken tiles. The teachers, as if herding sheep, follow behind shouting, "Quickly now" in rhythm with the museum guards' constant reminders not to touch anything.

The students finally shuffle into the last hall where the Buddha statues are on display. Recently, the Samhwaryŏng Buddha Triad was spread out against one wall of this room. Unlike the crowded displays of the previous rooms, the triad occupies a spacious area. (Indeed, this is how museum exhibits ought to be displayed). No longer distracted by excessive exhibits, the crowds gradually gravitate to the triad, where they eye the baby-faced Buddhas with their mirthful smiles. Soon one of the children exclaims, "Look at that!" and the room is filled with chatter, "Oh, it's so cute! It's just like a baby!" The teacher sternly shouts "Quiet!" but her voice drowns in the hum of excited voices.

An aesthetic response naturally seeks release. Applauding at the end of a music recital is just one example. And after all, there's no need to repress one's sense of astonishment at the Baby Buddhas' charm. Occasionally, there is even a student so entranced by the statue that he or she remains standing there in spite of the teacher's remonstrations. Just as we cannot resist the temptation to pat the head of a cute child whom we pass on the street, the children would love to be able at least to touch the figures' hands. But they are fenced off by a rope and in the corner, there's also a very official-looking man wearing a hat. Even so, when the guard turns around for a moment, some of the bolder students manage to reach in and touch the statues. Without time to caress a hand or face, they hastily touch the toes. The oil from the fingers of the little rascals has built up over the years, turning the toes black.

The Familiar Image of the Niche Buddha

In studying history in school, Koreans hear time and again about the 'brilliant culture'. We also learn (in tedious fashion) about the numerous invasions that ravaged our county, as well as the moral decadence and reckless extravagance of the ruling class. Yet whenever culture is mentioned, we are told that it was brilliant. This contradictory depiction of Korean culture is either the result of blind patriotism or the inferiority complex of a culture that has at times been less than brilliant.

Actually, if we look at the history of any country, there are ups and downs. In addition to times of greatness, there are periods characterized by mediocrity. Within the vast cycles of birth and decay, cultures rise from periods of decline, go through a process of preparation, achieve a renaissance and enter periods of brilliant creativity—only to fall prey to complacency, over-consumption and confused cultural values.

In the early seventh century, during the reigns of King Chinp'yǒng and Queen Sǒndǒk, Shilla gained complete confidence in its ability to create works of art from its own perspective. While open to influence from the neighboring cultures of Paekche, Koguryǒ and China, it now had the ability actively to assimilate borrowed cultural elements into its own unique culture. As an example of this, there is the well-known story about Grand Master Wonhyo. While on his way to study in China, he suddenly decided to turn back. Although he never studied abroad, he went on to develop his own philosophical system. In a sense, this event marks a turning point in Shilla history, when the kingdom had gained confidence in its own culture. From this point on, it was felt that one could learn whatever one wished without traveling to foreign lands.

A similar example of this can be found in our own times. During the 1950s and '60s, any Korean intellectual studying the social sciences felt a sense of inferiority, or at the very least, was a bit apprehensive if he or she had not studied overseas. But by the '80s and '90s, attitudes had changed to the point that overseas study was no longer felt to be necessary. On the contrary, it was believed that a scholar should encounter the actual circumstances of his own native country and work to integrate both his life and studies in the concrete reality surrounding him. Wonhyo, who grew up during the reign of Queen Sǒndǒk, was also affected by a culture that was beginning to assert its own independence.

The Buddhist statues that are thought to date from Queen Sǒndǒk's reign also reflect Shilla's sense of cultural pride. One of the best examples of this is the Niche Buddha on the northern foot of Mt. Namsan. Its genial, benevolent expression may be attributed to the fact that it is a representation of the Buddha, but it also has a warm, familiar air as if the sculptor had used a Shilla maiden as the model. In its own way, this masterpiece of classical Shilla art reflects the legacy of Wonhyo, who popularized Buddhism by creating a unique Korean synthesis of its teachings.

Of the thousands of historical relics in Kyŏngju, this Niche Buddha always makes me feel at peace. I don't know how many times I have stood before this image, entranced by its bounteous expression of earthy compassion. This Buddha is one of Kyŏngju's top sites, yet I would have a difficult time explaining how to get to it. The lack of signposts or other markers shows how poorly some of Korea's cultural sites are maintained. In terms of location, it is about a thirty minute walk on the mountain behind the museum, but it would be nearly impossible for the average person to find it using a tourist map. The best way to get there is to ask a taxi driver to take you to the entrance of Ongnyong'am (Jade Dragon Hermitage). This area, locally known as T'apkok (Pagoda Valley), contains a group of Buddhas in relief. Sculpted during the pre-unification Shilla period, these artifacts are of great interest to art historians because of their diverse iconography portrayed in a rough, antiquated style. They should definitely be included in any field trip to Mt. Namsan. Next to T'apkok lies Pulgok (Buddha Valley) and half way up this valley, one finds the Niche Buddha.

When I first tried to find my way to the Niche Buddha, I asked directions at the three-way intersection in front of T'apkok. No one seemed to know what I was talking about. Finally, I came across a lady who said she had heard about it. Saying that it wasn't famous, she suggested that I visit T'apkok instead. I then came across an old man from the local village. Pointing westward, he told me that when I came to a 'dog farm', I should head up the mountain. Following his directions, I did indeed find a remote farmhouse and a barn. From there, I could see the museum in the distance beyond a stream. Worried that I would get lost, I carefully made my way from the house until I came to a marble

NICHE BUDDHA IN MT. NAMSAN'S BUDDHA VALLEY
This Buddha, sitting inside a niche carved from natural stone, looks like a friendly lady supervising a student boarding house.

slab with the words "Entrance to the Niche Buddha, 500 meters Ahead". I walked about 500 meters in the direction the arrow had pointed but was unable to find any more sign posts. I climbed up, down and to the side but found nothing. I even tried crossing to the other side of the stream. On that dreary autumn day, I wandered around for hours to no avail. I went back to the dog farm and asked the lady there for directions to the Niche Buddha. Although the lady had lived there for 20 years, she could only tell me that she'd heard something about such a place but had never been there herself. In the end, I failed to see anything but the sign. On the following day, I asked someone at Kyŏngju Museum's cultural bureau. I was told that I had to make a sharp right onto an obscure path about 500 meters from the sign. I therefore returned and walked up 500 meters from the entrance. After several hours of trying anything that even remotely looked like a path to the right, I finally found the Niche Buddha.

In spite of these difficulties, I could bear no grudge against this Buddha, nor did I pity it for the neglect it had suffered. To the contrary, this Buddha deserves our praise for having survived intact for over 1,350 years with the same contented expression. The rock from which it was carved was rooted deep in the earth, keeping it from the hands of looters, and the carved niche protected it from the elements. Since it wasn't a well-known tourist site, it remained untouched by dirty hands. Where else could we find such an unspoiled masterpiece that had changed so little since it was first carved? I was not the first person to stand enraptured before the image. A Japanese student told me that he had visited the image on a moonlit night and was so struck by it that he pitched a tent there and spent the night. When I look at this Buddha, it reminds me of some friendly lady in charge of a student boarding house. Although it is difficult for me to get away for a night, I have fantasized about coming during the full moon and spending the night with this Buddha.

The most sensible way to set up field trips to Kyŏngju is to divide one's itineraries according to cultural periods. Thus, the first trip would be to relics from Kyŏngju's tumuli period. By visiting Panwolsŏng and the royal tombs in chronological order, one could get a faint glimpse of the area's ancient past. The second trip would be to see the artifacts from the reign of Queen Sŏndŏk—the golden era of pre-unification Shilla culture. These would include the Hwangnyongsa Temple site, Punhwangsa Temple, Chŏmsŏngdae, the Samhwaryŏng Baby Buddhas, the Niche Buddha and King Chinp'yŏng's Tomb.

On the third trip, one could see artifacts associated with Unified Shilla's vibrant spirit as it consolidated its power over the former realms of Paekche and Koguryŏ. These artifacts would primarily include three-story pagodas, such as those at the Kamŭnsa, Kosŏnsa and Hwangboksa Temples as well as Yŏngji (Reflection Pond) at Pulguksa Temple. The fourth trip would be to see the harmonious, idealistic beauty of sites associated with the mid-eighth century—the heyday of Unified Shilla culture. These artifacts would include Pulguksa Temple, Sŏkkuram, Anapchi and Emille Bell. The final trip would be to the key sites on Mt. Namsan. Looking at the numerous rock sculptures and pagodas that dot the mountainside, one could witness the Shilla people's attempt to create a Buddhist Pure Land on earth. After completing these trips, one could take on the remaining artifacts site by site until one had finally conquered Kyŏngju.

I now sit in seat number 33 on my way back to Seoul. Having just completed a field trip to the artifacts from Queen Sŏndŏk's reign, I find the journey back much more significant. The bus goes through the Kyŏngju toll gate and enters the expressway. To my right, I can see Kŏnch'ŏn Railway Station and a short distance beyond this, a panorama of mountain ridges to my left. Within these mountains lies Yŏgŭn'gok (Woman's Root Valley) which resembles a massive close-up of a woman's

WOMAN ROOT VALLEY Situated at the foot of Mt. Pusan in Kŏnch'ŏn Township, this valley gets its name from its terrain features which resemble a woman's private parts. The area forms the background of a legend about Queen Sŏndŏk. During the Chosŏn Dynasty, it was said that any scholar who passed through this area on his way to Seoul to take the civil service exams would surely fail. When traveling through Kyŏngju towards Pusan on the Kyŏngbu Expressway, the valley can be seen off to the right after passing through the Kyŏngju Tunnel.

pubic area and thighs. The *Memorabilia of the Three Kingdoms* mentions this valley in connection with one of the queen's three prophecies. When the queen heard frogs croaking in the dead of winter at Ongmunji (Jade Gate Pond), she sent troops to Yŏgŭn'gok. There, they came across Paekche soldiers whom they surrounded and killed. The queen, when asked how she had been able to make this prophecy, said that since 'Jade Gate' was a common term for a woman's genitals, the Paekche troops would die. I haven't been there personally, but I've heard there is still a spring in the valley called Ongmunji. The valley looks particularly erotic in late winter when the first buds appear on the trees' dry branches. The queen's confident prediction of the death of Paekche troops just as the male sex organ 'dies' (goes limp) after male orgasm is perhaps an indication of her bold character. It was this very boldness that led to the wonders we see on the second tour itinerary mentioned above. I should probably conclude this chapter at this point, before I wander off on any more tangents. Those who would like to learn more about Queen Sŏndŏk should look at the passage towards the end of Book 1 of the *Memorabilia of the Three Kingdoms*.

August 1991

1.*Han'guksa t'ŭkkang* (Seoul: Seoul National University Press, 1990).

2.*Hanguk kwahak kisulsa* (Seoul: Chŏng'ŭmsa, 1975).

3 In English, sometimes spelled 'Emillie' or 'Emileh'.

4.*Samguk sagi.*

5.In East-Asian thought, *yin* and *yang* (Korean *ŭm* and *yang*) are the two opposite yet complementary forces behind all phenomena. *Yin* represents the feminine and passive principle, whereas *yang* represents the male, active principle.

6.*Samguk yusa.*

Ah, Kamŭnsa Temple and Stupa!

Kamp'o Kado / Taewang'am / Kamŭnsa Temple Pagoda / Sŏkka Pagoda

A LUMP OF STONE SPEAKS!

At the university, I teach Korean Art History. In addition to art history students, who take the course as part of their major, there are art students who take it as a course in theory, Korean history and philosophy students, etc., who take it as an elective within their majors and other students who take it as a general elective. As a result, I have to alter my lecturing style slightly to suit the particular group of students taking the course. This is especially true when it comes to showing slides.

Students from the humanities become excited and smile only after something has been explained and they have had the chance to mull it over for some time. When slides are shown to art students, on the other hand, they spontaneously respond with exclamations and laughter. In general, the aesthetic response of female students is quicker. For this reason, when I show slides to a mixed class of art and humanity students, there is usually a two-to-three second gap between their responses. This demonstrates the difference between the aesthetic response of the students, with female art students on one end of the continuum and male humanities students on the other. By the end of the semester, this lag in receptivity has almost disappeared. Even so, there always remain a few slow students.

One year, there was such a male student by the name of Inho in the Korean History Department in the College of Humanities. Inho's aesthetic receptivity was particularly slow, and to make matters worse, he had absolutely no confidence in his perceptive skills. When he was in my class, we went on an expedition to Kyŏngju. He stared blankly at each historical site we visited as if he had seen it all before. However when we came to the Kamŭnsa Temple Pagoda, his response to this ancient work was quicker than my own. He immediately exclaimed, "Look at this, sir, it is truly grand!" He was apparently a bit embarrassed at his outburst, for he then went on to explain, "For the first time in my life, I feel like a lump of stone is speaking to me." As he said this, he ran up to the pagoda, eyeing it from different perspectives and cheerfully rubbing his hands across the stone surface.

This is the power of the Kamŭnsa Temple Pagoda. After all, a true masterpiece requires no explanation. One simply contemplates the immediate impression and leaves it at that. It's like that moment in the World Cup soccer match between Korea and Argentina when the Korean team made a brilliant goal. The avid soccer fan experiences great bliss as he reflects on that unforgettable moment. If the editors of this book permitted me to write about my trip to Kamŭnsa Temple anyway I chose, I would fill the entire manuscript with:

"Ah, Kamŭnsa Temple and pagoda! Ah, Kamŭnsa Temple and pagoda! Ah, Ah, Kamŭnsa Temple...."

Inho or anyone else who visits the site even once will understand why I feel this way, but for those who haven't been there, I am burdened with the task of recreating that brilliant goal of the soccer match for those who slept through the game.

On the Path to Kamŭnsa Temple

What is the most beautiful path in Korea? The walk from Namwon along the Sŏmjin River to Koksŏng and Kurye is known for its great beauty, as is the walk along the Namhan River from Yangsu Village to Yangp'yŏng or the walk from P'unggi over Chungnyŏng, past Kudanyang to the Ch'ungju Dam. Among these scenic paths, it is difficult to say which is best. Of the walks I've taken, one of the most unforgettable is the gorgeous path from Kyŏngju to Kamŭnsa Temple, often referred to as the Kamp'o Kado (Kamp'o Highway).

This route skirts along the northeast side of Mt. T'ohamsan and through the twisting Hwangnyong Valley until it comes to Ch'uryŏng Hill. From the hill, one can see Taejong Stream and a wide plain. This route leads directly to Yongdangpo's Taewang'am (Great King Rock) on the East Sea.[1] Although a mere 30 kilometers long, it takes one past mountains, lakes, hills, valleys, a broad plain, a river and the ocean. In this sense, this scenic route provides a short introduction to the various types of Korean landscape. Autumn comes late to this area, which is especially beautiful during November.

In addition to lovely scenery, the area is full of history. While on a trip from Kyŏngju to Taewang'am, I looked out of the car window, reflecting on the area's numerous cultural treasures and their significance. These relics are over a thousand years old, but the path itself dates from an even earlier time.

Ancient Kyŏngju's 'downtown' area is thought to have been situated between Punhwangsa Temple and the Hwangnyongsa Temple site. Driving eastward through this area along Pukch'ŏn (North Stream), one passes the turn-offs to the Hwangboksa Temple Pagoda and King Chinp'yŏng's Tomb, after which the road winds up towards Myŏnghwal Fortress. You should keep looking out the right-hand window at this point. If you look out the left, you might be enticed by the den of Satan—otherwise known as the Pomun Tourist Resort Complex. Here,

THREE-STORY PAGODA AT THE KAMŬNSA TEMPLE SITE
As the basic model for subsequent three-story pagodas
of the Unified Shilla period, this pagoda combines
a solid-looking two-story base with the gradually
diminishing proportions of its three story body.
The structure thereby gives one a sense of both stability
and ascension.

countless hotels and various frivolous amusements bedazzle one's eyes. On Pomun Lake, large plastic swans float around as crowds of well-dressed tourists file past the cacophony of the vendors. One thing I hate about the resort is its lack of cheap lodging. When the resort was developed, only expensive hotels were allowed. In short, the resort caters only to those of means. Those who are less well-off need not even consider staying there. The place is a clear example of discrimination in regard to social class. In short, the Pomun Tourist Resort Complex is for the wealthy ruling class, designed for the 'hallowed-bone' or 'true-bone' aristocrats of the 20th century.[2]

Those who manage to ignore the glitter and look off to the right will see a pair of pagodas standing firmly on a flat plain. These mark the Chŏn'gun-dong temple site. The building next to them is Sŏrabŏl Elementary School. From this point, the road begins to climb, taking one past a cliff on the right. To the left, you can see a long reservoir known as Tŏktong Lake. Created in the 1970s as a part of Kyŏngju's development plan, the reservoir serves as a source of potable and irrigation water and helps control the water levels of Pomun Lake. Built by damming a valley, the lake runs up numerous small gullies. From the shore, it is impossible to see exactly where it ends and begins. Unlike typical Korean lakes with their cozy atmosphere, this lake has a dignified feeling. Looking at the broken shore line, one imagines the water endlessly winding back through small valleys.

Driving further up the incline, Tŏktong Lake slowly comes into full view. From here, one can see Amgok-dong on a hill in the distance. This area was home to Kosŏnsa Temple where the famous monk Wonhyo served as abbot. Mujangsa Temple once stood in this area also, but the only remains are a three-story pagoda and a broken stele base.

The stele that stood here was discovered during the reign of the Chosŏn-dynasty King Chŏngjo while Hong Yangho (styled Yigye, 1724-1802) was mayor of Kyŏngju. (At the time of discovery, the stele fragment was being used as a mortar to grind beans). The inscription is said to be that of the famous Korean calligrapher Kim Saeng or a follower of the Chinese master Wang Hsi-chih (307-365). The calligraphy of the inscription is magnificent. When hearing about it, the famous calligrapher Kim Chŏng-hŭi (styled Ch'usa) visited the stele to make a rubbing which he then took to show a renowned Ch'ing epigraphy expert.

The site serves as the background for a legend about King Munmu. According to the *Memorabilia of the Three Kingdoms*,[3] the king, following in his father's footsteps, drove the T'ang forces out of the Korean Peninsula and united the Three Kingdoms. In order to show that the national emergency was formally over, he buried a military helmet at the site. Thus the temple acquired its name, Mujangsa (Helmet Buried Temple). I think of this legend as the abolition of the militaristic culture that had developed during the battles for unification.

As the reservoir fades away in the distance, my imagination runs away to the sound of our car struggling up Ch'uryŏng Hill.

TAEJONG STREAM'S FALL FROM GLORY

Churyŏng Hill is quite high. From the top, one can see the East Sea sparkling through the white mist. The steep descent involves countless switchbacks and sharp curves. At the bottom of the hill, one suddenly comes across a deep, cool valley. If one continues through the rugged landscape, one comes to a musk-deer farm. For several years now, each summer has brought hoards of visitors to this valley. This is just another reason to visit in November. Coming out of Hwangnyong Valley, one comes to the wide plain of Changhang Village. Two small creeks meet here to form the large Taejong Stream. One of the creeks comes down from Mt. Hamwolsan, while the other trickles down the eastern face of Mt. T'ohamsan.

If one goes up the Mt. Hamwolsan stream, one comes to Kirimsa Temple which was founded during the reign of Shilla's Queen Sŏndŏk.

About one kilometer down the valley, one finds Kolgul Hermitage. There is a large relief carving of Buddha at the site, dating from the Unified Shilla period. This Buddha had a major face-lift several years ago. The figure has an expression that emanates perfect calm. Kirimsa Temple boasts a lacquered Bodhisattva statue made in 1510, charming Chosŏn-era temple buildings and a newly-opened museum. With so much to see, it must be included in any tour of the area.

Several kilometers up the Mt. T'ohamsan creek lies the Changhang Village temple site. To get there, one crosses a stream seven or eight times. This old temple site was one of the 'three things' that Sobul suggested had to be experienced in order to know Kyŏngju. At the site, there is an exquisite five-story pagoda and a destroyed stupa. During the Japanese occupation, the latter was dynamited by thieves who stole the sarira[4] reliquary. The only other relic at the site is a large Buddha statue base. With no custodian, the sole sign of life at this deserted site is the occasional brushing together of reeds. However, the place was alive with the spirit of a new age during the early Unified Shilla period (perhaps during King Munmu's reign) as Shilla worked to create a vibrant, new culture. Even now, while standing at the site, one can sense the great dignity of ancient Shilla temples.

Before long, I'm driving alongside Taejong Stream through a plain. Taejong is said to have been a large river in the past. Sea water apparently came quite a distance up the river, which is now a mere stream. This once-great river evidently faded into history along with the Changhang Village temple site, Kolgul Hermitage and Kirimsa Temple. As the Korean saying goes, "a wound leaves a deeper mark than glory." Unable to erase its troubled past, the stream keeps flowing onward.

In 1235, the Mongols launched three separate invasions into Korea, turning Kyŏngju into a sea of fire. At this time, the marauding warriors burned Hwangnyongsa Temple's Nine-Story Pagoda to the ground. They also made plans to cart the temple's bell back to Yuan China. However the bell weighed approximately 100 tons (four times as much as the Emille Bell), so the invaders eventually decided that the only way to move it was by sea. They therefore dragged the bell through this area and put it on a river raft, but the craft sank right before it reached the sea and the river eventually pushed the giant bell out into the ocean. As a result the river came to be known as Taejong(Large Bell) Stream. Residents of this area claim that, when the water is rough, you can still hear the bell tolling. From the Japanese occupation to the present, numerous attempts have been made to find this bell.

At the point where the sea breeze can be felt at the mouth of Taejong Stream, one finds the village of Ŏil within Yangbuk Township. At an inspection point here, soldiers stop and check cars. This always dampens the mood of a cultural outing, but this is only a preview of what's yet to come. The main feature is waiting for us at Taewang'am.

Leaving the road to Kamp'o, we take the right-hand road toward Yongdang village and Ponggil village. From here, the road heads straight towards Taewang'am at Ponggil Village. Yongdang Village can be seen at the end of a slope on the left, and at one end of the village, there is a pair of stone stupas. The only other thing found at this old temple site is a zelkova tree. This area was once underwater, so Kamŭnsa Temple— the monastery that once stood here—would have been situated right on the coast. Driving past the temple site toward the ocean, one can see Igyŏn-dae (Beneficial View Pavilion) off to the left and Taewang'am to the right. If the ocean were to dry up, it would take only about five minutes to walk to both places. From here, one can look out at the sea stretching towards the distant horizon.

After parking at Taewang'am, one looks down at Ponggil Village's black pebble beach. Here, the small stones perform a symphony as the waves push them back and forth. Only 200 meters away, one can see the waves breaking next to Taewang'am but, at this point, the first-time visitor is in for a great disappointment, for the path to the rock is blocked by a barbed-wire fence. I still haven't figured out whether this barbed-wire fence, which seems to surround all of South Korea, is really meant to keep out Communists or is merely used to instill fear in the general population. Yet I suppose we should be thankful. At least someone was thoughtful enough to provide a dog-sized gateway to crawl through. It saddens me to think that the beautiful and unforgettable tour route described above must terminate here. For this reason, when I'm guiding cultural tours, I often finish at Igyŏn-dae. Leaning on the rails of the pavilion, we can look over at the Taewang'am and the East Sea. This tour route is only 40 minutes by car, but with the wings of imagination, one flies through 1,000 years of history.

TAEWANG'AM: FACT AND FICTION

From ancient times, Taewang'am has been known as the place where King Munmu's ashes were scattered after he was cremated. The area was traditionally considered sacred and was therefore avoided by women divers who gathered shellfish and seaweed off the coast. Then one day, newspapers suddenly created a great commotion, saying that King Munmu's underwater tomb had been found here! Everyone accepted these reports, believing that something new had indeed been discovered. Before long, this 'new discovery' was listed in school textbooks and other works. A good example is the article on King Munmu in the *Grand Dictionary of Notable People.*[5] At the end of the article, we find the following:

> ...after his cremation, no one was sure where the grave site was located. In May 1967, however, the Shilla Five Peaks Research Organization[6] (managed by the *Han'guk Ilbo* newspaper) discovered a unique underwater crypt at Ponggil Village, Yangbuk Township, Wolsŏng County in North Kyŏngsang Province in which the king's remains had been interred.

TAEWANG'AM AS SEEN FROM THE BENEFICIAL VIEW PAVILION Hong Yangho, who served as mayor of Kyŏngju during the reign of the Chosŏn King Chŏngjo, performed a ritual here in gratitude for King Munmu's patriotism.

Not only was this untrue, it was a bit of a scam. After all, everyone in related research fields already knew this, but the mass media was given the impression that something new had been discovered.

There is probably no one who loved Taewang'am or knew so much about it as Ko Yusŏp (styled Uhyŏn). In 1940, Uhyŏn wrote "The Sea I Cannot Forget"[7] and "A Short Account of a Trip to Kyŏngju".[8] In these writings, he claimed that while the sea was always lovely, the coast near Taewang'am at Yongdangp'o was absolutely unforgettable. Uhyŏn tells his readers, "If you go to Kyŏngju, you must experience King Munmu's legacy." He mentions "Admiral Yi Sunshin who mastered the seas and Chang Pogo who enjoyed the seas" but concludes that it is King Munmu who should be remembered as a great patriot, the king, on his deathbed, vowed to become a dragon of the East Sea in order to protect the nation against Japanese invasions. In spite of this reference, Ko Yusŏp is not to be credited with the discovery of the tomb.

About two centuries ago, around 1796, Hong Yangho (1724-1802) served as mayor of Kyŏngju. When Hong visited Taewang'am and Igyŏn-dae, he heard the legend of the rock. Hong then compared the legend with related passages in *Historical Records of the Three Kingdoms,*[9] and concluded that this was where the king had been buried. According to his work *Collection of Yigye's Writings,*[10] he then gave a ritual offering in order to pay tribute to the king's great deeds. This is not the only old mention of the king's tomb. In the "Chiriji" Kyŏngju section of the *Veritable Records of King Sejong*[11] one finds the following statement:

> About 70 paces below Igyŏn-dae, there is a rectangular rock that rises out of the ocean. This is the burial site of King Munmu.

Going back to still earlier records, in the passage on the twenty-first year of King Munmu's reign (681), in the *Historical Records of the Three Kingdoms*, we find the following:

> The King passed away on the first day of the seventh lunar month...In accordance with his last wishes, his funeral was held at a large rock at an East Sea port. It is said that he transformed into a dragon so as to defend the nation. The rock was therefore called Taewang'am (Great King Rock). In his last testimony, the king said,...[an elaborate grave] will merely waste the nation's finances, result in books full of lies and create public hardship...Ten days after I die, cremate my body in the palace courtyard in Indian [Buddhist] fashion.

In the 'Flute to Calm Ten-Thousand Waves' Chapter of the *Memorabilia of the Three Kingdoms*, King Munmu gives his son, King Shinmun, a flute.

Munmu says that if his son blows on the flute, Japanese marauders will be repelled, rain will come in times of drought and diseases cured. In this chapter, we find the following passage:

King Shinmun...ascended the throne on the seventh day of the seventh lunar month in 681. He had Kamŭnsa Temple constructed on the east coast in memory of his father King Munmu. According to the temple records, King Munmu started construction of this temple in order to ward off Japanese invaders. King Munmu passed away before he completed this project and became a sea dragon. His son, King Shinmun, ascended the throne and completed the temple in 682. Under the steps of the Main Buddha Hall, there is a hollowed out area on the eastern end where the dragon can enter and coil itself up. Apparently, the place where the king's cremated bones were buried in accordance with his death will is called Taewang'am, the monastery is called Kamŭnsa Temple and the place where the dragon was later seen is called Igyŏn-dae.

Thus, the site of the king's internment is even mentioned by the *Memorabilia of the Three Kingdoms.* If this is the case, what is all this fuss about a new discovery?

DICTATORSHIP, MASS MEDIA AND CULTURAL TREASURES

What the 'Shilla Five Peaks Research Organization' claimed as a 'new discovery' was not the site where King Munmu's ashes had been scattered, but rather a crypt where his remains were supposedly enshrined. The Organization claimed that the four rocks of Taewang'am had been specially carved so that the waves would break over them. They pointed out that there was a small pool and a stone, shaped like a tortoise shell, in the middle of the rocks. Furthermore, they claimed that this stone, measuring 3.7 meters by 2.6 meters and 1.45 meters thick, was the tomb's covering stone. In addition, they speculated that there would be a chamber where the ashes were enshrined below the rock cover. Notice that this was merely an unproven hypothesis.

However, nothing was found beneath the tortoise-shaped rock. In spite of this, no one bothered to turn over the rock and make a thorough excavation of the site. It was impossible to tell whether the cuts in the rocks were natural or man-made. Even if the rocks had been carved, they would have been so eroded by the waves of the past 13 centuries that they would have looked natural by now.

This 'new discovery' becomes even less credible when we look at the fragments from King Munmu's stele, which were discovered by Hong Yangho. The fragments, in complete agreement with the accounts of the *Historical Records of the Three Kingdoms* account, say that "wood was stacked for the funeral" and "his bones were broken up and tossed in the sea." In spite of this, the Taewang'am tourist sign boasts that this is the only underwater grave in the world! At the very end of the signboard, there is a short statement that "some scholars claim that this is merely the site where [King Munmu's] ashes were tossed into the sea." I suppose we should be thankful that this is mentioned at all.

How did all this happen? First of all, the Organization's desire for scholarly achievement overcame their sense of scholastic modesty. Second, the mass media's sensationalism made a mountain out of a mole hill. In the end, the media zealously pursued the story for its commercial value without any thought of its truth. From its very inception, the Organization was not really a society for academic excavations and research. In reality, it was a commercial venture by newspapers who used famous scholars in their search for a 'story'. Third, the government dictatorship worked behind the scenes to control and manipulate the mass media and intelligentsia. In order to justify its *coup d'etat,* Park Chung-hee's government rewrote historical textbooks so that they glorified military heroes. In particular, historical accounts related to the rule by the military during the Koryŏ period and Yi Sŏnggye's founding of the Chosŏn Dynasty were embellished. Needless to say, the government was especially fond of talking about King Munmu's militaristic spirit. Simple-minded scholars completely fell for this ruse. By the time of the Third Republic (1962-1976), this attitude had led to tremendous self-alienation among scholars.

When Taewang'am was 'discovered' in May 1967, it was presented in a special one-page feature by all the newspapers. It just so happened that this was right before the most rigged election in Korean history. This was eventually followed by measures to change the Constitution so that the dictator could stay in power indefinitely. During the unfavorable political environment of the period, the dictatorship was doing all it could to distract the population with non-political events. Yellow papers such as *Sunday Seoul* and *Chugan Han'guk* appeared at this time. This was back in the days when an elephant sneezing at Ch'anggyŏngwon Zoo in Seoul would make the society pages. The Third Republic also used the excavation of the Ch'ŏnma-ch'ong (Heavenly Horse Tomb) and the following international exhibition to divert attention from its numerous excesses and justify its rule.

Gazing at Taewang'am, I cannot help but feel upset. I watch the endless waves beat against this rock where flowers never grow. As a symbol of military culture, the rock reminds me of the daily struggle of progressive intellectuals and the tough lives of the common people.

Below Igyŏn-dae, the road branches off towards Kamŭnsa Temple and Taewang'am. At the corner of the intersection, Uhyŏn's disciples have erected a rock with the inscription 'The Sea I Cannot Forget'. Whenever I make a cultural tour to Kamŭnsa Temple, I make a point of stopping here. I always think to myself, 'Master Uhyŏn, whom I so deeply respect, the great legacy of King Munmu which you sought after has now come to this. Your inscription should be changed to say: Instead of searching for King Munmu, go to Mujangsa Temple.'

"THE SEA I CANNOT FORGET"
Inscribed with the title of
a collection of essays by
Ko Yusŏp, the stone reflects
Ko's passionate interest in
art history.

THE IDEA BEHIND THE STONE PAGODA

King Munmu wanted to erect a Buddhist temple at this port of access to Kyŏngju, but his death in 680 prevented him from doing so. His son, King Shinmun, seeking to realize his father's dream, set to work on the temple and finished it in 682—a year after ascending the throne. Built out of gratitude towards his father, the monastery was named Kamŭn-sa (Gratitude for Kindness Temple). Since King Munmu had vowed to become a dragon and protect the area after he died, his son created a hollow space in the floor where the dragon would be able to enter. This hole can still be seen in the old temple site's foundation.

With a single Buddha Hall and twin pagodas, the temple seems to have been a tranquil place that lacked excessive architectural flourishes. This same design was later used at the famous Pulguksa Temple near Kyǒngju. The pair of three-story pagodas seems to be the progenitor of the traditional three-story pagodas popular during the Unified Shilla period—a style which found its greatest expression in the Sǒkka Pagoda at Pulguksa Temple.

When looking at history, there is a tendency to evaluate it according to its highest achievements. In the study of art in particular, we tend to focus on fully developed masterpieces from a culture's golden age. However, it seems to me that the initial emergence of a form is just as significant. Likewise, later innovations, which eventually lead to the overthrow of a fully developed art form, cannot be overlooked. After all, the developed art form may possess refined beauty, but it generally lacks the imposing power of initial forms. At the same time, it does not have the revolutionary creativity or inventiveness of art forms that later appear to challenge it.

This is evident when we compare the grave, classical Phidiansculptures of the earlier Classicism in the ancient Greek Art with the smooth, bright Praxitelean sculptures of the later classical period. Likewise, it is clear when we compare the phonetic Korean script (Hunmin Chǒngǔm) as written when invented by King Sejong with the refined calligraphy in *Illustrations of Stories Exemplifying the Five Confucian Virtues*[12] made under the reign of King Chǒngjo.

Whereas China and Japan are respectively known for brick and wooden pagodas, Korea is the country of stone pagodas. When Buddhism first entered Korea via China, wooden pagodas were popular. Subsequently, large structures such as Hwangnyongsa Temple's nine-story wooden pagoda were constructed. Later, Paekche artisans developed stone pagodas based on these early wooden structures.

The two nine-story structures at the Mirǔksa Temple site in Iksan are the earliest examples of stone pagodas in Korea. Although made of stone, they are actually imitations of wooden pagodas. These early structures were eventually simplified to form their own unique style. For example, the five-story pagoda at the Chŏngnimsa Temple site with its base, square sections for each story, roofs and finial represented another fully developed architectural form distinct from its predecessors. Whenever I make a trip to Puyŏ, I end up standing for a long time in front of this pagoda, which strikes me as an ideal, formal expression of elegance.

Ko Yusŏp, in his major work *Research on Chosŏn Pagodas*[13] provides detailed analysis of the Chŏngnimsa Temple Pagoda. He discusses how it instigated a transformation in Buddhist thought from an emphasis on both pagodas (stupas) and Buddha Halls to an exclusive focus on the Buddha Hall as the central place of worship. He also talks about issues surrounding the time of completion, the structure's preservation and construction materials. However, the question that I personally find perplexing is why this structure, which played a seminal role in the development of stone pagodas, was constructed in Paekche and not in Shilla or Koguryŏ. My thoughts on this are as follows. The Mirŭksa Temple and Chŏngnimsa Temple Pagodas were constructed around 600 C. E., which would have been during the reign of Paekche's King Mu. This was the period when Paekche culture had attained its greatest development. The famous gilt-bronze image of Maitreya sitting pensively with legs half-crossed was created at this time as well as the Buddhist rock carving at Sŏsan. During this period, Paekche fully assimilated the highly developed Buddhist culture of China and went on to produce its own unique works and culture using the country's natural environment and materials. In particular, it took advantage of Korea's ample supply of hard granite to create artistic works such as the rock carvings at T'aean and Sŏsan, the stone Buddhas at Yesan and Chŏng'ŭp and stone pagodas. However, Paekche's culture went into a decline at this point.

A PANORAMIC VIEW OF KAMŬNSA TEMPLE SITE *The design of this temple, which consists of a single Buddha Hall and a pair of pagodas, became a model for later Unified Shilla temples.*

Unified Shilla thus became the heir to the legacy of the Chŏngnimsa Temple Pagoda.

BIRTH OF THE THREE-STORY PAGODA

The five-story pagoda at Chŏngnimsa Temple became the model for later Shilla temples. Examples include the five-story pagodas in Ŭisŏng's T'ap Village, Wolsŏng's Nawon Village and Changhang Village. By the time Kamŭnsa Temple was constructed, the five-story pagoda had been reduced to three stories. Why were the structure and number of stories changed?

This development must be explained in terms of a stylistic analysis. The Chŏngnimsa Temple Pagoda is very elegant and refined. I suppose the term 'noble' best captures it. Yet it somehow lacks force. The body of the

first story stands tall, invoking a sense of the transcendent, but its small base does not seem to provide firm stability.

Kamŭnsa Temple's construction reflected the vibrant mood as the people of Unified Shilla set about constructing a new nation from the former Three Kingdoms. The elegant but frail looking five-story pagoda did not suit the national mood. This new era called for a solemn and dignified structure, something that looked stable and strong. The new style had to somehow combine transcendence with a sense of stability. In artistic terms, however, transcendence and stability are normally contradictory. If an art object is tall, it seems transcendent, yet unstable. If it is made squat in order to emphasize its sense of stability, it seems less transcendental. During the Unified Shilla period, this dilemma was solved by clearly distinguishing between the pagoda's base and body. Stability was expressed in the base, while transcendence was expressed in the pagoda's cheerful, tactile rhythms.

The Kamŭnsa Temple Pagoda's base consists of two levels of tightly-stacked stone blocks. The body of the first story briskly rises, while the second and third stories gradually become smaller. These diminishing proportions draw one's eyes towards the structure's finial, which is in a direct 80-degree line with the roofs of the third, second and first stories as well as with the outer edge of the base. This feature prevents the solid-looking base from weakening the transcendental effect. As the basic model for subsequent three-story pagodas, this structure represents a significant innovation.

When the Kamŭnsa Temple Pagoda was erected, Korean artisans were attempting to create works that were magnificent and imposing. A century later, the focus switched to elegance and refinement. For this reason, this structure is the tallest three-story pagoda in Korea. It stands 13 meters high, and even if the 3.9-meter-long metal finial is excluded, still comes to an imposing 9.1 meters. The structure's sense of ascension is not exaggerated but is solidly grounded by the wide and stable base.

My knees always get weak as I stand awestruck in front of this pagoda. The structure's imposing force must have been what my student Inho felt when he said, "I feel like a lump of stone is speaking to me."

The Kosŏnsa Temple and Sŏkka Pagodas

As mentioned before, the Kamŭnsa Temple Pagoda became the prototype for stone pagodas of the Unified Shilla period. This pagoda and the Kosŏnsa Temple Pagoda (constructed around the same time) were the two masterpieces of the early Unified Shilla period. Kosŏnsa Temple, where Grand Master Wonhyo served as abbot, was situated in Amgok-dong. With the creation of Tŏktong Lake, the area was flooded,

THREE-STORY PAGODA AT THE KOSŎNSA TEMPLE SITE
Kosŏnsa Temple is where Grand Master Wonhyo served as abbot. With the grandeur characteristic of early stone pagodas, this structure boasts an awe-inspiring beauty.

and the pagoda had to be moved to a corner of Kyŏngju Museum grounds. Here, most people walk right past the structure, unaware that it is a great masterpiece of the Unified Shilla period. On a typical day, you can see groups of people getting their pictures taken in front of the mock-up Tabo and Sŏkka Pagodas. The general lack of appreciation for the Kosŏn Pagoda is not so much due to people's ignorance as it is to the fact that Korean museums have not done enough to educate visitors.

In terms of scale and shape, the Kosŏnsa Temple Pagoda is similar to that of Kamŭnsa Temple. Both temples have the same sense of imposing majesty. However, the Kosŏnsa Temple Pagoda does not have a *ch'alchu* (pole adorning the top) and the lines and angles are a bit softer.

Whenever I lead a cultural tour to the pagodas around Kyŏngju, the group ends up discussing their impressions on the monotonous bus ride home. On one such trip, there was an older single lady. In our previous discussions, she had made it clear that she had no intention of marrying, so we were all a bit surprised when she said the following:

> The Kamŭnsa Pagoda, in all its perfection, elicits feelings of profound respect. Yet if I were to chose a partner, I'd rather have a man like the Kosŏnsa Pagoda. Instead of perfection, this pagoda embodies compassion and inclusiveness.

Art historians, who generally concentrate on chronicles and formal development in their research, could learn a great deal from this lady. With an acute appreciation of art, she has already acquired the basic methodology required for the study of art history.

Eighty years after the Kamŭnsa and Kosŏnsa Temple Pagodas were erected, the three-story pagoda reached its acme with the construction of the Sŏkka Pagoda. Situated at Pulguksa Temple, this exquisite structure harmoniously combines elegance, refinement and nobility. In terms of scale, the Sŏkka Pagoda has been reduced to two-thirds the size of the Kamŭnsa Temple Pagoda. Yet, instead of looking diminutive, the structure seems to have an appropriate size. Almost everyone who sees Kamŭnsa Temple Pagoda says that it looks bigger than they expected. Due to the pagoda's large dimensions, the builders were unable to make the first story with a single stone. Instead, four stones were used as pillars and the hollow spaces were then filled in with small stones while flat panels were placed on the exterior. As a result, the pagoda now houses a number of snakes. I always warn my students that, if they climb onto the pagoda to pose for a picture, they might end up with a pair of fangs in their leg. Of course, they all assume that I've concocted this whole story just to keep them off the monuments. However, one student who ignored my warnings and sat stretched out along the base got quite a shock one day when a snake suddenly stuck its head out from between a pillar and one of the panels. Snakes also live in the Kosŏnsa Temple Pagoda.

TOURING WITH SOBUL

On a spring night in 1985, I went with Sobul to Pulguksa Temple. I had told him that I wanted to see the Sŏkka Pagoda in the moonlight. Since then, whenever I think of the temple, I remember the way it looked that night.

On the way back home, we stopped at the Kyŏngju Museum and looked at the three-story pagoda from the Kosŏnsa Temple site. I felt ecstatic as I looked at this structure, which possesses grandeur lacking in the Kamŭnsa Pagoda. At that time, Sobul turned to me and said:

"The Kosonsa Temple's stone pagoda seems to be alive. When seen from far away, it doesn't look like anything special but, as you approach it, it seems to expand gradually. Standing directly in front, one feels overawed by it. Take a close look."

"When I look at this pagoda, it reminds me of a movie star. It's like Sophia Loren."

"I see. How about the Sokka Pagoda?"

"With such a noble and aristocratic air, it would have to be Grace Kelly, don't you think?"

"Listen to this guy! You've got it all wrong. Grace Kelly could never be so graceful. The Sokka Pagoda is no other than Ingrid Bergman in *For Whom the Bell Tolls*."

Thinking back on myself describing beauty in terms of Western movie stars, I realize how deeply my generation has been affected by the cultural imperialism of the West. But what can be done about it now?

SŎKKA PAGODA AT PULGUKSA TEMPLE This could be called the paragon of beauty. In this structure, the three-story pagoda of the Unified Shilla period attains its full development.

During my young and impressionable years, I was deeply influenced by Western cultural icons. Even so, I don't think I have ever seen a beauty that compares to the Kamŭnsa Temple Pagoda. This structure's charm, so difficult to approach and grasp, seems truly unique. I felt in a similar way when I first heard Gregorian chants, the traditional ritual music at Chongmyo (Royal Ancestral Shrines) and Buddhist nuns chanting in a seminary at Unmunsa Temple. Such a sublime beauty is rarely met with in this world. Ah, the Kamŭnsa Temple and Stupa!

September 1991

1. Sea of Japan.
2. The hallowed-bone and true-bone were ranks within Shilla's bone rank system (*kolp'um*). Originally, only those of the hallowed-bone status could become king but, after the disappearance of this rank, those of the true-bone rank occupied the throne.
3. *Samguk yusa.*
4. Sarira are small gem-like remains left over after an enlightened master or person of great purity is cremated. The most famous sarira are those from the Buddha.
5. *Inmyŏng taesajŏn* (Seoul: Shinkumunhwa-sa).
6. Shilla Oak Chosadan.
7. Naŭi ichiji mothanŭn pada.
8. Kyŏngju kihaeng iljŏl.
9. *Samguk sagi.*
10. *Yigyejip.*
11. *Sejong shillok.*
12. *Oryun haengsil to.*
13. *Chosŏn t'app'a-ŭi yŏn'gu.*

Emille Bell:
Old Legends and New Facts

King Sŏngdŏk's Divine Bell / Moving the Bell from Pongdŏksa Temple /
The Later-Heaven Opening Dance / Park Chung-hee Bell in Pulguksa Temple

A SOUND SOLEMN AND PURE

Up until several years ago, the Emille Bell was rung at six every morning to announce the new day. The sound it made when struck has been the same since the 14th day of the 12th lunar month of 770 when it was first placed in its belfry.

I visited the bell a day after Sobul insisted that I had to hear the Emille Bell to understand Kyŏngju. At six on a late autumn morning, I stood there in the frosty air listening, for the first time, to the bell being struck. Breaking the dawn silence, the sound had a deeply solemn air. When hit, there was initially a low tone, followed by clear and long reverberations that echoed into the distance. It seemed like the most marvelous instrument in the world.

Typically, if bells have a low, solemn ring, the sound is not clear, and vice versa, but the Emille Bell somehow managed to combine these two traits. As Sobul once said, although the bell has this tremendously loud sound, it is a sound as lucid and pure as the morning dew.

This joining of contrary aspects to form an artistic synthesis may be said to represent the high point in Unified Shilla culture. It also demonstrates, in a concrete manner, the ancient aesthetic ideal of harmony. This

155

synthesis of opposites can be witnessed in many of the era's artifacts. Three-story pagodas such as the Kamŭnsa Temple Pagoda and Sŏkka Pagoda combine a sense of loftiness and stability, while Anapchi utilizes both straight lines and curves. The exquisite synthesis of the man-made and the natural in Korean art is yet another example. The Emille Bell, likewise, combines various qualities. When struck, the sound is both solemn and pure. In a similar manner, the design gives one a feeling of reverence and elegance.

As with most bells, the Emille Bell is roughly in the form of an inverted paper cup with the lower section expanding outward, but with the very bottom subtly curving back inward. In terms of design, this helps maintain a sense of dynamic tension. Typically, art objects that look solemn and imposing lack grace and vice versa; yet the Emille Bell manages to incorporate these two characteristics. For this reason, I don't feel that the word 'beautiful' does justice to the bell. To me, it is sacred. It is a divine bell with the greatest form and tone that man can create and is worthy of the greatest praise and respect.

FAILURE TO MAKE REPLICAS IN THE TWENTIETH CENTURY

Overcome by emotion after hearing the Emille Bell for the first time, I aimlessly walked up through the high reeds at Panwolsŏng to the west of the museum. On the one hand, I felt a great deal of gratitude, and on the other hand, sharp pains of remorse. The gratitude was to our ancestors who made this bell, while the remorse was due to what it revealed about the dullness of modern society and cultural practices.

Almost everyone who visits Kyŏngju ends up going to the Kyŏngju Museum. And most visitors also stop and look at the Emille Bell across from the entrance. What thoughts go through their minds? What do they feel after they leave? They probably remember the horrific story about how a child was sacrificed to make the bell. And they perhaps calmly reflect on the embossed fairy motifs and elaborate arabesques. But do

they actually sense the bell's greatness?

Probably not. In this age of scientific achievement, the techniques used to make such a bell do not seem in the least impressive. Most people today would lightly praise the artisans for producing such a work 12 centuries ago. However, I would like to firmly state that such a bell can no longer be made. The Emille Bell was without precedent and will never be reproduced.

In 1986, two attempts were made to replicate the bell. One of these, dubbed the 'Friendship Bell', was a gift to America for the bicentennial of its foundation. It now sits in a Los Angeles park next to the Pacific Ocean. In 1987, I spent ten months in America. During this time, I went up to the bell and secretly struck it. It sounded as if I had hit a tin can. Externally, it was a copy of the Emille Bell, but it completely lacked the original's solemn and elegant tone.

The other copy was put at Poshin-gak (Universal Trust Pavilion) in Seoul. Having become too old to use, the original Poshin-gak bell was placed in the back courtyard of the National Museum. On this copy, the ancient designs of the Emille Bell were modernized in an awkward fashion. Most importantly, the copy didn't sound anything like the original.

Every year on December 31, bells ring in the new year. Both the Poshin-gak Bell and Emille Bell are struck at this time. On live television broadcasts, the Poshin-gak Bell (or more accurately, a copy of the Emille Bell) appears first, followed by the Emille Bell. No matter how tone-deaf a person may be, one can instantly distinguish between the real bell and its imitation. The fake Emille has a clanging metallic sound, while the real Emille has (as its inscription says) a 'solemn perfect sound'.

How do we explain this? In terms of technology, our society is a million times more advanced. Why can't it recreate a bell made 12 centuries ago? There is only one explanation: our age cannot imitate the attitude and spirit of those who made the Emille Bell.

In the 20th century, numerous replicas of the Emille Bell have been produced. When producing these copies, manufacturers have been obsessed with copying the bell's external design. The idea that a bell should have a beautiful sound has been almost totally ignored.

The makers of the Emille Bell, on the other hand, were deeply concerned with the bell's tone. This is particularly evident when we look at the bell's inscription (over 1,000 characters long), which begins with the following passage.

> Profound truth includes invisible phenomena. Thus even though one looks, one cannot see it. Even though its thunderous sound pervades the space between Heaven and Earth, one cannot know the source of its echo. For this reason, [the Buddha] taught the truth using appropriate similes in accordance with the time and the listener. Likewise, the sacred bell was hung so that [living beings] could hear the perfect sound of truth.

The bell's ringing thus represents 'the perfect sound'. The Buddha's words, when put down in writing, became Buddhist Sutras; his appearance, when replicated, became Buddha statues; and his voice was represented by the ringing of bells.

It seems to be a general principle of human history that when the spirit of an age dies, it is never reborn. In our age, we can manufacture cars and computers, but have completely lost the ability to duplicate something like the Emille Bell. For that matter, we cannot even preserve it properly.

Why has the Emille Bell, which tolled for 12 centuries, suddenly fallen silent? Even now, the Emille Bell has nothing wrong with it. There is not the least sign of a crack or fault. The authorities in charge of Korea's cultural assets have decided that the best way to preserve the bell for all posterity is not to use it. The Venerable Wolsan at Pulguksa Temple is of a different opinion. "A bell must be struck to keep it from rusting. It's just like anything else, when its function disappears, its life is cut off." At present, even the block of wood used to strike the bell has been removed so that the Emille Bell truly looks like an old relic sitting in a museum. To borrow an expression from a famous French critic, it now sits in "a cemetery for masterpieces."

FROM PONGDŎKSA TEMPLE TO THE MUSEUM COURTYARD

The Emille Bell stands 3.7 meters high. It is 7 meters in circumference, 2.27 meters wide at the bore, 22 centimeters thick at the bottom and 10 centimeters thick at the top. With approximately 3 square meters in total volume, the bell weighs around 22 tons. This mammoth project was completed on the 14th day of the 12th lunar month in 770.

The bell was initially housed in a belfry at Pongdŏksa Temple, a monastery especially devoted to King Sŏngdŏk (r. 702-737). As a place where monks would regularly pray for the repose of the king's soul, it was a natural site for the bell. At present, we no longer know the exact location of the temple. All we know is that Kyŏngju's Puk Stream flooded at one point, destroying the temple, and the bell was found among the debris. Kim Shisŭp (1435-1493, styled Maewoltang)[1] wrote his work *Legends of Mt. Kŭmosan*[2] while living at Yongjangsa Temple on Kyŏngju's Mt. Kŭmosan (Mt. Namsan). The work includes the following poem describing the devastation at Pongdŏksa Temple.

Pongdŏksa Temple has been buried in a field of stones,
Its bell hidden beneath the grass.
Children toss rocks at it
While cattle use it to sharpen their horns.
Did this ever happen to the stone drums of Chou?[3]

According to the *Revised Edition of the Augmented Survey of Korean Geography*,[4] Kim Tam hung the bell next to Yŏngmyosa Temple in 1460 while he was serving as mayor of Kyŏngju. This work goes on to say that Ye Ch'unnyŏn, who served as mayor in 1506, constructed a belfry at Ponghwang-dae outside of Kyŏngju's south gate. He had the Pongdŏksa Temple Bell moved to the new belfry, where it was struck when the city gates were opened and closed and during military assemblies. As the largest Shilla tumulus, Ponghwang-dae is 22 meters high and 82 meters in diameter. In later years, people, having forgotten that it was a tomb, assumed it was just a hill. As a result, it came to be known as Ponghwang-dae (Phoenix Heights).

Yŏngmyosa Temple was a large monastery. It is famous for the legend about the young man who fell in love with Queen Sŏndŏk. However, the location of the temple and the reason for moving the bell are no longer known. Records mention that fires were a frequent problem, so the temple may well have gone up in flames.

In August 1915, after spending 480 years in a belfry below Ponghwang-dae, the bell was moved to the old Kyŏngju Museum behind the Kyŏngju

A 1915 picture of the Emille Bell being moved from Ponghwang-dae to the old Kyŏngju Museum (Courtesy of the DongA Ilbo).

Courthouse. (This area originally had been the city's administrative district.) There is an old photo showing the bell being moved to its new site.

BUY TEN ROLLS OF WHITE COTTON

From early spring to June 1975, the Emille Bell was moved to the new site of the Kyŏngju Museum. An account of the move can be found in an article written by Sobul for the November 1985 issue of the magazine *Han'gugin.* The events that Sobul recorded are a great cause for shame.

At the time, Sobul, who was serving as curator of the Kyŏngju Museum, made every possible effort to ensure that the bell was transported safely. After all, this sacred bell was something that modern man could no longer produce. Sobul felt that it would be an unforgivable crime were this priceless work to be damaged through carelessness.

Taehan T'ong'un, a Korean transport company, took on the job of moving the bell to the new museum. The Emille is 3.7 meters high and weighs 22 tons. After being packaged for transport, the crate stood 5 meters high and weighed 30 tons. When it was hoisted up onto the truck trailer, it stood 6 meters high. The trailer and the bell's combined weight came to 50 tons.

The distance from the old museum to the new one is no more than 2 kilometers, but there was a bridge along the way, and it was decided that the structure could not support 50 tons. For this reason, the movers were forced to take a circular route through the city. Unfortunately, the city's electrical wires were too low. However, there was no other choice. So numerous workers from Korea Electric Power Corporation were called out to cut the wires in front of the bell and to reconnect them after it had passed through.

When the bell was prepared for removal, a monk from Tudae Village in Wolsŏng County performed the traditional Buddhist rites. Having heard that the bell was to be moved, the citizens of Kyŏngju all gathered in the plaza in front of train station in the morning to watch the spectacle. The crowds were huge. Kyŏngju presently has around 130,000 residents, but at that time had a population of 100,000. Everyone in the city seemed to be at the station.

When the truck carrying the bell passed by, the entire crowd began to follow it. Everyone seemed determined to accompany it all the way to its destination. Sobul had not expected this festive parade which suddenly formed behind the bell, but an idea occurred to him. He ordered to buy ten rolls of cotton cloth. He took the cloth and attached long streamers to the bell, which the crowds could hold as they marched behind. Before long, this spontaneous gathering had turned into a giant parade. Sobul led the parade in the front car, going at a leisurely enough pace so that even the eldest could follow. As the electricians cut and reattached the overhead lines, the bell was paraded through the city. In the end, it took two hours to go the 5 kilometers.

Strangely enough, I have not been able to locate a single photo of this event. A television reporter is said to have come, but purportedly left when no one was willing to give him a gratuity to film the event.

Lend Me a 28-Ton Ingot

Sobul had transported the bell to its belfry at the new museum, but he now had to worry about suspending it. In particular, he had to make sure that the new belfry had been constructed properly. He was worried that the construction workers might have been overconfident in their knowledge of modern technology. Most of all, there was the possibility that the metal ring holding the bell would break.

In order to put his worries to rest, Sobul asked Pohang Iron & Steel Company for a 28-ton ingot that he could use to test the ring. His request seemed absurd. The steel company had never exported unprocessed ingots, and the price of sending such a large mass of metal was considerable. Yet, Sobul kept repeating how this was for the Emille Bell and how the 'Sacred Bell of King Sŏngdŏk' was a unique cultural relic that could never be replicated. After several days and countless conversations, the company management was finally persuaded. In Korean society, even the impossible becomes possible if you know the person in charge. As it worked out, one of the top people at the steel company had gone to high school with Sobul. Thus, after much difficulty, the Pohang Iron & Steel Company lent Sobul a 28-ton ingot. Taehan T'ong'un, a transport company, conveyed the ingot free of charge while others, such as the heavy machinery specialists Yi Yong'il and Operations Chief Kim Ch'angbae, donated their time for free.

Sobul had asked for 28 tons, thinking that the extra 6 tons would cover any margin of error; however, this was a mistake. Since the bell might sway in the wind, its support actually had to be twice as strong. Thus 44 tons were actually needed properly to test the metal ring's ability to hold the bell. Having discovered this fact too late, Sobul shook the ingot repeatedly throughout the day. The construction foreman, on the other hand, felt that the trial was excessive since the ingot weighed 6 more tons than the bell. In spite of the foreman's reservations, Sobul went out every time he had a chance and moved the ingot back and forth to simulate the striking of the bell.

On the morning of the seventh day, a museum guard ran up to Sobul

The 28-ton ingot that Sobul, then the curator of the Kyŏngju Museum, borrowed from Pohang Steel Co. to test the bell clasp is being lowered back down to the ground.

and informed him that the bell's ring was bending open. On the tenth day when it was clearly on the verge of breaking, the ingot was lowered to the ground. Sobul was trembling as he pulled off the bent ring and looked at it. Placing it in a box, Sobul took it to Seoul where he showed it to other experts and bureaucrats associated with the Emille Bell project. The chief of the Office of Cultural Properties, the president of the construction company, the museum curator and the head of the Korea Atomic Energy Research Institute assembled in the curator's office in the National Museum to discuss the problem. Together, they formed the Emille Bell Ring Manufacturing Committee to ensure that the Emille Bell project was concluded without any mishap.

THE EMILLE BELL RING MANUFACTURING COMMITTEE

The committee consisted of various scientists such as Kim Yusŏn (a member of the Korea Atomic Energy Research Institute) and Hwang Ch'anggyu (a metalwork expert), as well as Sobul and various museum experts. As its first course of action, it had the bent ring tested at a machinery company in Inch'ŏn. Looking at the test results, the company researcher informed them that it was made of "crappy metal".

The ring wasn't the only problem. The clasp that was fastened to the ring also had to be able to support 22 tons. Mr. Hwang said that the clasp should be made of special steel at a well-qualified factory that he knew of. The clasp could be made according to his specifications, at least 15 cm in diameter. He felt completely confident that such a clasp would never bend or break.

There was, however, a major hitch. The ring at the top of the bell was dragon-shaped, with a 9 cm space beneath the dragon's belly. However, a 15 centimeter-wide space was needed according to modern theories of dynamics. After struggling with the problem, Mr. Hwang finally concluded that modern technology offered only one other solution. Numerous strands of wire could be wound through the ring. Yet, it was

THE EMILLE BELL CLASP
The gap beneath the
dragon's belly is big
enough for a clasp
8.5 cm in diameter.
Since modern technology
is unable to produce
such a small clasp with
sufficient strength,
the old one has been
used unmodified.

obvious that a ball of wire would look a bit odd at the top of this ancient treasure.

Then one day, Mr. Hwang turned to the curator and asked, "Sir, does the original clasp still exist?" Sobul promptly took it out of the storage room and showed it to him. Mr. Hwang was elated, "This will hold the bell safely!" According to modern technological knowledge, nothing smaller than 15 cm would work, yet he was telling us this smaller clasp was safe. Hwang went on to explain. The old clasp, which could have been made as early as in the Shilla or as late as the Chosŏn period, was produced from a long plate of alloy metal, which was pounded flat and then rolled up. By doing so, the final piece was able to combine the dispersed force of the metal—just as wire would. When metal objects are strong, they tend to break easily, and when they're flexible, they tend to stretch out. The old clasp overcame this dilemma. Although strong, the metal would not break or stretch.

Thus, the committee failed to make a new clasp for the bell.

As mentioned before, twentieth century man is no longer able to produce a replica of the Emille Bell. This is not merely due to a lack of earnestness, for our technology is also insufficient. Although we can make computers and cars, our knowledge of bronze casting actually lags behind that of ancient times. Seen in this light, scientific method and the accumulation of technological knowledge sometimes seem to represent mere change rather than 'progress'.

On the body of the Emille Bell, there are two circular lotus designs on both sides, situated on the same axis as the dragon head on top. The bell only emits its proper sound when struck solidly on one of these lotus designs. All the other designs and patterns, including the fairies, introductory inscriptions and verses, decorative nubs on the upper section and arabesque designs, are symmetrically placed to the left and right of these two designs.

As Dr. Yi Changmu from Seoul National University's College of Engineering likes to point out, the same batter striking at the same pitch can hit either a home-run or a foul. It all depends on where the bat meets the ball. Likewise, the two lotus designs are points where the bell must be hit to produce a 'home-run'.

In February 1963, Ko Chonggǒn and Ham Inyǒng (two Ph. D.s working at the Korea Atomic Energy Research Institute) took gamma ray transmission photos of Buddha statues and bronze bells from the Three Kingdoms period. They presented their scientific findings in the eighth and ninth issues of *Art Materials* (*Misul charyo*). The two researchers could not understand how artisans of the period had produced such thin castings or how they had produced metal without air bubbles. Like other bells from the period, the Emille Bell is free of air bubbles.

There have been a number of scientific studies on the bell. Dr. Nam Chǒnu, in his famous work *Rediscovering Historical Artifacts,*[5] conducted a scientific examination of Korea's bronze bells. Along a similar line, Dr.

Yŏm Yŏngha wrote about the technical skills and other aspects of bronze bells in his work *Studies on Korean Bells.*[6] To a non-scientist like myself, the bell simply strikes me as a great enigma (as do the writings of physical scientists).

According to Dr. Nam Ch'ŏnu, the bell was created using the lost wax casting technique. This differs significantly from the ceramic mold casting and centrifugal casting techniques used in China and Japan. In fact, Chinese and Japanese scholars typically employ the phrase "the Korean bell" in their writings, recognizing that the particular casting techniques used in Korea produced a bell that was distinctly different in terms of both design and tone. Indeed, intricate designs as well as the lingering reverberations after the bell is struck can only be produced using the lost wax casting technique.

Several years ago, Tsuboi Ryohei, a Japanese scholar specializing in bronze bells, put together a program for NHK—a Japanese television station. During the program, he compared the musical quality of bronze bells throughout the world and concluded that the Emille Bell was clearly the best. Explaining his choice, he mentioned the bell's solemn, clear tone and echoing vibrations.

In the terminology of physics, when Korean bells are struck, the phenomena of 'interference' occurs whenever two sound waves of roughly the same oscillation arise simultaneously. However, it is not yet clear why this effect occurs with the Emille Bell. Some people think it may have something to do with the tall protuberance behind the dragon-shaped ring on top. This hollow column of metal stands 96 centimeters high. This hypothesis seems even more likely in light of the fact that this column is not seen on Chinese and Japanese bells.

I visited the bell one morning, determined to solve the mystery of the lingering vibrations. After striking the bell, I quickly crawled underneath it. To my surprise, the trailing hum wasn't audible from inside. I then wanted to try sitting inside while the bell was struck, but I was a bit

The Emille Bell
With a majestic and clear
tone, the bell has beautiful
curves that combine elegance
with artistic tension.

worried about ruptured eardrums (Sobul would have no part of it). But I would still like to try this little experiment if I ever get the chance.

According to Dr. Nam Ch'ŏnu, to create the Emille Bell using the lost wax casting technique, it would have required 22 tons of molten metal, or actually 25 to 30 tons to account for the 20 to 30 percent loss during casting. The inscription says that 120,000 *kŭn* were used. If a *kŭn* is calculated at 225 grams, 27 tons were used.

When 27 tons of molten metal are poured into a container, the metal exerts tremendous pressure, which will break all but the strongest molds [according to Dr. Yŏm Yŏngha's research, marks on the bell indicate that molten metal was poured into ten different places on the mold] to make matters worse, air bubbles often appear during the pouring process and become trapped as the metal hardens. How did the artisans get rid of these air bubbles? Cast metal works of the present are full of bubbles; yet ancient works such as the Emille Bell are free from them. When we try to fathom how such a bell could have been made, it is truly a mystery!

THE EMILLE BELL LEGEND

Originally known as the 'Divine Bell of King Sŏngdŏk', the Emille Bell acquired its current name from its sound. Its lingering vibrations sound like 'emille' which means 'because of my mother'. The legend behind the name is as follows. King Kyŏngdŏk sent a monk throughout the nation to collect money for the casting of the bell. When the monk arrived in one village, a lady with a child in her arms teased the monk, "We have nothing to give except this baby." Later, after several attempts to cast the bell had failed, an official diviner concluded that there was an impure influence which could only be eliminated through a sacrifice. After much searching, the impurity was attributed to the woman. Her infant was thus put into the cauldron of molten metal, becoming a part of the 'Emille' Bell.

To some, this legend expresses the hardships of the people who were coerced into donating for the project. Others believe it refers to the collective efforts of everyone in the nation, down to the smallest child. Whether or not a child was actually sacrificed is still debated.

Those who say the child was really sacrificed point out that the chemical composition of the baby's bones could have played an important role in the casting. The phosphorus in human and animal bones has a peculiar ability to bond materials together. Since ancient times, it has also been known to help bond metal alloys. For a similar reason, the first emperor of China is said to have used corpses when he built the Great Wall. Evidently, the decomposing bones helped harden the foundation. Another example is Pyŏkkolche (Blue Bone Dike) built in Kimje during the Samhan period. It is said that every time the dike was built, high tides would wash away its base. As typically happens in Korean legends, the head of construction had a dream in which he received a revelation from a divine spirit. The spirit told him to mix 'blue bones' with the mud used to build the dike. Since animal bones, and particularly horse bones, normally have a bluish tint, horse bones were ground up and used in the construction, which turned out to be a success.

Those who deny that the sacrifice took place claim that the story is merely a mythological fabrication. Regardless of the value of phosphorus, such a small amount thrown into 27 tons of molten metal would have no effect whatsoever. Moreover, the story's mention of a single cauldron is absurd, as it would have taken more than 100 vessels to hold the molten metal.

Two Thousand Bee Hives Are Required

I find it interesting that the bell's echoing sound is the topic of the legend, and that people from that era tried to explain it by means of a story. If all bells had a lingering tone as beautiful as the Emille's, this legend would never have been formed. Its mysterious sound comes from its unique construction, for it was the first bell successfully made from lost wax casting.

Inscriptions on the outside of the bell provide details related to its creation. King Kyŏngdŏk (r. 742-764) paid 120,000 *kŭn* in order to have a giant bell constructed in his father's memory. Unable to finish the project personally, King Hyegong left the work to his son, who completed it in the seventh year of his reign (771). The bell was then placed in Pongdŏksa Temple.

Why did this bell take so long to make? Fifteen years before the Emille Bell project began (754), the kingdom was able to make a bell four times as large (500,000 *kŭn*) for Hwangnyongsa Temple and a Medicine Buddha three times as large for Punhwangsa Temple.

According to Dr. Nam Chŏnu, the Emille Bell took longer due to the period of trial and error as the kingdom switched from the centrifugal casting technique to lost wax casting. The manufacturing date (14th day of the 12th lunar month) provides further evidence of this. To use wax casting, there first had to be bee's wax. Since the Emille Bell has a volume of three square meters and a single bee hive yields only 1 to 2 liters of wax, at least 1,500 to 2,000 bee hives would have been required. Needless to say, this is a very tall order. The biggest natural honey producer in Korea, located at Hwangi Village on Mt. Sŏraksan, has around 279 hives. Hives for the Emille Bell would have been gathered around the ninth lunar month and in the following month, the wax would have been shaped into a mold.

Even after the bell was removed from the mold, the casting would have still been incomplete since touch-up work had to be done (Evidence of this can be seen on the inside of the bell). This supplementary work was probably meant to give it a clearer tone. When the bell was subsequently hung and struck for the first time in 771, the virtues of lost wax casting could be heard in the bell's echoing tone. Those present must have marveled at the new sound, overjoyed at their success. Trying to describe the tone, some of those present may have claimed that it sounded like the word 'Emille', yet it was officially known simply as the 'Divine Bell'.

In the inscription, we find the following:

> The completed bell stands tall as a mountain, while its tone is like a dragon reciting poetry. Its sound echoes to the end of the sky and below the earth. May all who hear it be blessed with good fortune.

THE LATER-HEAVEN OPENING DANCE WITH THE EMILLE BELL AS ACCOMPANIMENT

The Emille Bell's lovely tone has always struck me as something found nowhere else in the world. I have often tried to conceive of a dance that would go with its melody. In May 1986, I actually had the opportunity to try this. When Oh Yun's engraving exhibition opened at the Min Gallery, Yi Aeju performed the commencement *kut* (shamanic dance), while I lectured on his art under the theme of 'Issues Surrounding Folk [Art] Forms'. After listening to my lecture, Yi said that if I put together a slide show on the unique features of Korean art, she would perform a corresponding dance routine. We thus created the 'Meeting of Dance and Art' for the 40th anniversary of Seoul National University.

When the university got wind of the plan, they froze funding for the project in an attempt to stop it. This was during the latter part of the Fifth Republic (1980-1988) when anything even slightly resembling 'folk' or 'people's' art was thought to be subversive and was therefore suppressed. Refusing to bow to these pressures, we went ahead with the project using funds provided by Kim Yongt'ae and Sŏng Wan'gyŏng. Most of this money paid for the musicians' transportation. I therefore asked Yi Aeju to limit the accompaniment to a percussion quartet and music from a cassette player. Immediately assuming a serious expression, she sharply criticized the idea. Essentially, her argument was that a dancer made her living by dancing to music. How could she be expected to dance to the spiritless and lifeless music from a tape? She went on to say that good music was needed for good dancing. How could someone who supposedly knew art suggest such a thing? After her scolding, I was utterly ashamed and embarrassed. I felt that I had to do something to make it up to her. So, as things were finishing on the last day of our performance, I casually made a proposal, asking her if she would care to dance to the best music in the world. When she asked what that was, I told her, "The Emille Bell".

I had good recordings of the bell—copies I had obtained from Sobul. Listening to the bell for nearly a decade, Sobul had discovered that the trailing sound was different in each season, and was especially long and clear on summer nights. However, there was a problem with the recordings. As soon as the bell was hit the first time, all the toads and frogs in the area would start croaking. So we had the people in the area go out and throw stones into the rice paddies. After the chorus of frogs and toads stopped, we were able to make the best recording of the bell. Yi Aeju, after listening to the bell being repeatedly struck, agreed to try dancing to it.

To myself, I was thinking that I was in deep trouble. I'd made the offer half-heartedly, thinking she would certainly refuse. Since she'd accepted, I now had to worry about Sobul. Would he go along with the idea? At any rate, the words were already out of my mouth, and it did strike me as something worth trying. So I headed down to Kyŏngju and gave Sobul a detailed explanation of the plan. This was before Yi Aeju had become famous for her performance of the *Parammaji* Dance[7], so Sobul only knew that she was a professor at Seoul National University. In response to my request, Sobul flatly told me I was talking nonsense and firmly stated that such permission could never be granted. People had to get permission merely to photograph this national treasure and I was expecting to strike it!

But I am a stubborn person. During my life, I have often heard people say that I'm as "headstrong as a cow spirit." I therefore pestered Sobul until he was finally persuaded. But Sobul consented only under the following conditions:

October 3 is Kaech'ŏnjŏl (Heaven Opening Celebration). The Shilla Cultural Society will hold an official ceremony at this time, during which the bell will be struck 33 times. This represents the opening of the 'Heaven of the Thirty-three'. If someone comes and dances in an unofficial capacity at this time, I will pretend not to know about it. Only ten people from Seoul who have a real need to see the dance may come.

When I got back to Seoul, I boasted to Yi Aeju that I had succeeded.

Yi's expression became serious. While the New Year's Eve celebration might be acceptable, she felt that the Kaech'ŏnjŏl celebration—only a fortnight away—did not give her enough time to prepare a performance.

I explained this to Sobul, but he insisted that the dance could not be part of an official public performance and must therefore be done on Kaech'ŏnjŏl. He would allow no changes. Left with no other course, I went back to Yi Aeju and pestered her until she agreed to do the dance on Kaech'ŏnjŏl.

Yi Aeju thus prepared her performance. Sobul invited Yun Kyŏngnyŏl,[8] while I invited traditional music scholars Ch'oe Chongmin and Kwon Osŏng, art history scholars Yi T'aeho and Kang Kyŏngsuk, Korean history scholars An Pyŏnguk and Yu Sŭngwon, art scholar Sŏng Wan'gyŏng, movie director Chang Sŏnu and an acquaintance of Sobul.

However, Yi Aeju suddenly canceled just two days before the performance, saying that she did not have enough time to prepare. She said that with only the sound of the bell to go by, it would virtually be an unaccompanied performance. She wanted to postpone until next year. After so much effort, the whole plan seemed doomed.

I went to Kyŏngju to give Sobul my deepest apologies. Sobul was also sad, saying that this would probably be the last opportunity for such a performance. I was to find out later that Sobul was to be transferred from his job as curator at the Kyŏngju Museum to a position in Seoul.

In a last ditch effort, I tried to broker an agreement between Yi and Sobul to have the performance on October 9. Yi Aeju agreed, but Sobul insisted that we had no right to strike the bell at that time.

I suggested that Han'gul Day served as a good excuse to ring the bell, which could be struck once for each of the 28 Han'gul letters created by King Sejong. Since the bell was struck three times each morning anyway, this would bring the number to 31. It then seemed fair to ask that it be struck just two extra times to fit in with Yi Aeju's performance.

Thus, at 6 a.m. on October 9, 1986, Yi Aeju performed the Huch'ŏn

At 6 a.m. on October 9, 1986, Yi Aeju performs the Later-Heaven Opening Dance to the accompaniment of the sound of the Emille Bell being struck.

Kaebyŏngmu (Later-Heaven Opening Dance) for ten invited guests and twenty-odd members of the Shilla Cultural Society.

From the thirty guests, groups of four took turns striking the bell at one-minute intervals, which were slowly reduced to thirty second intervals. After it was struck for the third time, Yi appeared in a white traditional dress, slowly approaching through the bell's lingering echoes. She clutched a folded bundle of white cotton cloth. After circumambulating one time, she reverently placed the cloth in the concave pit under the bell as if making an offering. Each time the bell was rung, she would repeat rhythms and pauses. Her tragic movements would alternate. At times, she seemed to sob, pray, leap with joy, or assume an attitude of defiance or respect. As the bell's tempo quickened, she reached beneath the bell and grabbed one end of the cloth and cheerfully glided away. As the last lingering hum of the bell ended, she faded away in the distance with the long line of cloth trailing behind her. For more than twenty minutes, the thirty spectators had been speechless as they listened to this ancient sound and watched this modern dancer.

Yi Aeju returned to applause. Yun Kyŏngnyŏl wanted to know this dancer who was daring enough to perform in front of the Emille Bell. Although he knew something about the art, he said he had never imagined there could be a dance that would fit so well with the Divine Bell of King Sŏngdŏk.

Unfortunately, nobody took a video of this performance. From the beginning, everyone had expected the director Chang Sŏnu to film the event, but he couldn't come. Ironically, Chang had already rescheduled his October 3 filming for October 9 so that he could come to the show. Thus, the bell once again avoided video cameras, as it had done during its relocation.

After the performance, we all went to eat at the P'arujŏng Rotary. On the way, Sobul turned to me and said.

"The Emille Bell seems to have some karmic affinity with cotton cloth.

When we moved it, ten rolls were used, while two rolls were used in the dance."

"It seems to me that it isn't the bell's karmic affinity but the dead baby's."

"How's that?"

"The cloth that the mother bought for the baby's diapers and wrap were never used."

"So you agree with the theory that the baby was sacrificed!"

"Sure."

PRESIDENT PARK CHUNG-HEE'S SACRED BELL AT PULGUKSA TEMPLE

Most people have now forgotten about it, but a bell on the scale of King Sŏngdŏk's Bell was forged during our times.

Sometime during the 1970s, a bell was hung at Pulguksa Temple. At the most, it was one-fourth the size of the Emille Bell. Part of the inscription says, "We pray that President Park Chung-hee will enjoy long life. Donated by Cho Chunghun of the Hanjin Group". This, then, may be called the 'Divine Bell of Park Chung-hee'.

This bell was always hanging at an angle, like a clock hand showing 6:05. Although it is still used as the temple bell to announce the morning and evening chants, it has a hollow sound that quickly dies out.

The Venerable Wolsan at Pulguksa Temple was always disturbed by this, so he asked the Kyŏngju Museum to come examine it. The museum's research team found that the thickness was at fault. Unlike the Emille Bell, which is 10 cm thick at top and 22 cm at bottom no matter where one takes the measurement, Park Chung-hee's Divine Bell was 10 cm thick in some spots and 5 cm in others. It was full of air bubbles, and one side was so thin that it should have been transparent. Its awkward angle and hollow sound were therefore to be expected.

Just as I'm not sure about the Emille Bell's legend, I don't know what this 'Divine Bell' has to do with Park Chung-hee's assassination on

October 26, 1979. But one thing is clear. When I visited Pulguksa Temple in the autumn of 1982 two years after Park's death, the inscription had been rubbed off. And the bell was hanging at 6:00 sharp.

October 1991

Note: After the first edition of the Korean version of this book, numerous people contacted me with information about pictures of the bell being moved. At the photography exhibit 'Taking Another Look at Kyŏngju's Museum,' numerous photos of the bell were shown.

1. Kim, along with Yi Maengjŏn, Cho Yŏ, Won Ho, Sŏng Tamsu and Nam Hyoon, was one of the famous six loyal ministers who gave up their official posts and refused to serve under King Sejo who usurped the throne of young King Tanjong.
2. *Kŭmo shinhwa.*
3. A Chinese dynasty associated with classical Chinese culture.
4. *Shinjŭng tongguk yŏji sŭngnam.*
5. *Yumurŭi chaebalgyŏn* (Seoul: Chŏngŭmsa, 1987).
6. *Han'guk chong yŏn'gu* (Seoul: Koryŏwon, 1988).
7. *Parammaji* Dance was performed by Yi Aeju desiring political democritization in 1987.
8. Author of *Namsan* and renowned Kyŏngju expert.

PART 3

Sŏkkuram

Mt. T'ohamsan's Sŏkpulsa Temple: A Glorious and Ignoble Past

Legend of the Temple's Foundation / Chŏng Shihan's Travelogue /
Resident-General Sone's Plundering / Dismantlement and
Reconstruction of Sŏkkuram

WHAT CONSTITUTES A WORLD-CLASS CULTURAL TREASURE?

One day, I received a very presumptuous phone call from a middle-aged lady. Having read my travelogue, she said she wanted to meet me and ask some questions. It all seemed a bit bothersome. Not wanting to waste my time, I coldly told her to ask me over the phone. In a ringing voice, she then stated her question.

I'd just like to say I can understand it when someone says that our culture is unique. Yet, I still suspect that such a statement actually comes from our nationalistic fixation on ourselves. I've been able to travel around overseas frequently with my husband and I have never come across anything like the Mayan temples, Egyptian pyramids, Roman Colosseum, Indian Taj Mahal or the Forbidden City of China. When I compare these world-class treasures to Korean artifacts, the latter seem so shabby. I'd like to hear what you have to say about this.

Unable to see the woman's face, I couldn't quite imagine her attitude. On the one hand, she sounded a bit haughty and proud; but at the same time, she reminded me of someone making a painful confession. Korea's middle-aged generation had grown up admiring Western culture. This question, which I had heard so often, thus seemed only natural. I responded, "You are right. Of course, Korea has no pyramids and no Taj Mahal." I went on.

But is Korea the only country lacking these things? Does France or Japan have them? The Mayan temples, after all, only exist in the former Mayan empire. So why do you look only at the top cultural treasures from around the world and get upset, when Korean artifacts fall short? Such a comparison is terribly unfair. What nation or people could live up to such high standards?

During the course of my pointed response, the woman didn't say a word. Having heard her mutter "uh-huh" several times, I imagined her head nodding in full assent. But a moment later, she said in a low voice, "I'm embarrassed to have put forth such a foolish question, but let me ask just one more thing. Does our country have a world-class cultural treasure?"

"Of course. First of all, there is Han'gŭl, the Korean alphabet, not to mention the Emille Bell and the Korean Tripitaka. Most important of all, there is the stone grotto known as Sŏkkuram. Even if all other Korean cultural treasures were to disappear, the nation's cultural pride would not be damaged one bit as long as Sŏkkuram remains."

"Is Sŏkkuram really that magnificent? Last summer I went there with the kids, and I wasn't so impressed. Maybe it was because we only got a glimpse of it through the glass. In your second book, you're going to write about the cave, aren't you? I'll make sure to read it and then go back and visit again. And...."

"And what?"

"If you can, tell your readers about my silly questions. Because a lot of the people I know feel the same."

After hanging up the phone, I felt bad. I really should have been thankful for her faith in me. If I could do it over again, I'd invite her for a cup of tea and have a good heart-to-heart talk....

A UNION OF RELIGION, SCIENCE AND ART

At some point, the *sŏkkul* (stone grotto) at Sŏkpulsa (Stone Buddha Temple) came to be known simply as Sŏkkuram (Stone Grotto Hermitage). This sculpted cave is a magnificent work. Indeed, I sometimes fear that my attempts to reduce this great achievement to words amount to little more than arrogance.

Sŏkpulsa Temple's stone grotto is an artistic masterpiece combining religion, science and art. In the cave sits an impeccable depiction of the Buddha—the ideal human figure representing the realm of the absolute. In ancient times, people all over the world sought such an image of human perfection. Even today, people are awestruck when they stand in front of this Buddha. Able to say little more than "beautiful," they find themselves speechless. Yet within this silence, it is possible to hear a mysterious and solemn harmony that echoes from the infinite depths of the heart.

Sŏkkuram originally contained 40 figures, including a Buddha, Bodhisattvas, Arahants and apsaras (fairies). The attendant figures are situated around the central Buddha figure as in Buddhist cosmology. In a sense, this cave serves as a summary of the entire Buddhist canon; but as of yet, no scholar has been able fully to interpret the significance of this exquisite mandala.

Sŏkkuram was carved using techniques of tremendous precision and it structurally exhibits exact scientific detail. At the same time, the builders were attentive to the philosophical significance of each part, which was made to agree with other sections, as well as the overall composition of the work. Dr. Nam Ch'ŏnu conducted a survey of the cave and concluded

A VIEW OF THE GROTTO'S INTERIOR Sŏkkuram boasts a majestic iconography with the main Buddha figure in the center and 39 other figures, including those along the wall and the niche figures above.

that in the carving of the massive stone, the margin of error was less than 1 millimeter per each 10 meters. Put another way, the degree of accuracy exceeds 99.99 percent. Such painstaking accuracy is hard to imagine even in the modern age. In the 20th century, we have even failed properly to repair and preserve the image. Unfortunately, our excessive faith in modern technology has led us to ignore the scientific knowledge of the past.

Sŏkkuram's main figure is clearly a religious work of art. This cold, lifeless stone, which has somehow been endowed with eternal life and the image of the absolute, is the product of an artistic spirit filled with religious devotion. The statue's value as art is beyond dispute. Even the harshest critic ends up standing dumbfounded before this exquisite masterpiece. Likewise, poets have also found themselves at a sudden loss for words when trying to describe its mysterious beauty. The famous writer and poet Ko Ŭn summed it up well when he said, "All Korean adjectives of praise gathered there, but were then used, one by one, to describe other things. Thus it is impossible to find an adjective with which to give [the stone grotto] ample praise."

For this reason, I am only able to talk about the impressive cooperative effort that created this wonder. If I could add just one thing, it would be to say:

Those who haven't laid eyes upon it cannot talk about it since they haven't seen it. Those who have laid eyes upon it cannot talk about it since they *have* seen it.

So from here on, my words are a mere description of Sŏkkuram's glorious and ignoble history. On the one hand, I hope to provide testimony to those who have worked to bring this mysterious masterpiece to light or have devoted their lives to preserving this world-class artifact. On the other hand, I hope to describe the degradation of the site in the wake of twentieth century Korea's turbulent history.

Kim Taesŏng and the Temple's Foundation Legend

The only ancient reference to Sŏkpulsa Temple's foundation is found in the *Memorabilia of the Three Kingdoms*[1] in the section "Taesŏng who demonstrated his filial piety to the parents of two lifetimes." It is strange to find only this single mention about such a great work. To make things even more confusing, the author (Iryŏn) introduces two divergent sources, admitting that he himself cannot tell which one is correct. The first was an ancient record called "Kohyangchŏn", while the second was a manuscript known as the "Sajungki" (Temple Records). Moreover, Iryŏn, in his typical fashion, simply records this legend—a story which strikes the modern reader as somewhat dubious. Yet we must keep in mind that the events recorded in the *Memorabilia of the Three Kingdoms* are historical records of great exactness and credibility. In order to understand the full significance of the account, we must look for key symbols and metaphors. Only by doing so can we take off the mysterious veil that shrouds Sŏkkuram.

In the small village of Moryang-ni, also known as Puunch'on (Floating Cloud Village), a poor woman named Kyŏngjo gave birth to a son. With a big head and a forehead as flat as the wall of a fortress, the boy was called Taesŏng (Big Wall). His mother was too poor to raise him, so she sent him to work as a farmhand of the wealthy Pogan. In return for his labor, Taesŏng was given a small plot with which to earn enough for food and clothing. About that time, Chŏmgae, a virtuous monk from Hŭngnyunsa Temple, visited the house of Pogan and asked for a donation for the Six Wheels Ceremony at Hŭngnyunsa Temple. Pogan gave him 50 rolls of cloth. Chŏmgae proclaimed to Pogan, "A donor who rejoices in giving is always protected by celestial deities. For each thing given, he receives

10,000 benefits and is sure to live a long and peaceful life."

Upon hearing this, Taesŏng ran and told his mother, "Standing at the door, I heard a monk say that, for each thing given, one receives 10,000 benefits. It occurs to me that we are now poor because we failed to perform any good works in our previous lives, and if we do not donate now, we will only be that much poorer in the next life. Shall we donate our small farming plot for the ceremony so as to receive future merit?" As Taesŏng's mother approved, the plot was donated to Chŏmgae.

Shortly after, Taesŏng died. That night, a voice from heaven was heard above the house of Kim Munyang, the Prime Minister, saying, "Taesŏng, the boy from Moryang-ni will be reborn into your family." In great astonishment, members of the household went to the village only to find that Taesŏng was indeed dead. In the same hour as the heavenly announcement, the Premier's wife conceived, and in due course gave birth to a boy. The child kept the fingers of his left hand tightly clenched until seven days after his birth. When he at last opened them, it was seen that he held a gold medallion inscribed with the characters for Taesŏng. As a result, he took on his old name and his mother [from his previous life] was brought into the wealthy man's house to be taken care of.

Having grown into a strong young man, one day, Taesŏng went to Mt. T'ohamsan where he killed a bear. Afterwards, he dreamt that the bear turned into a spirit and told him, "Why did you kill me? When I am reborn, I will kill and eat you." Trembling with fear, Taesŏng begged for forgiveness. The spirit said, "Then could you build a temple for me?" Swearing that he would do so, Taesŏng suddenly awoke to find his bed soaked with sweat. After this time, Taesŏng forbade hunting in the area. In the place where he had killed the bear, he built Changsusa Temple. Out of profound compassion, he built Pulguksa Temple for his current parents and

Sŏkpulsa Temple for the parents of his previous life and invited monks Shillim and P'yohun to stay at these temples.

The monk Iryŏn tells us that the above account is from the "Kohyangchŏn". He goes on to say, "Installing magnificent Buddha images, Taesŏng achieved great merit. He thus demonstrated filial devotion to his parents of both present and previous lives—a rare achievement even in ancient times. The 'cloud bridges' (stone staircases) and stone pagoda's exquisite stone and wood carvings at Pulguksa Temple are unparalleled in all the temples of the eastern region." Iryŏn then goes on to provide a different account that had been passed down in the temple records.

According to the "Sajungki", "Taesŏng, First Minister during the reign of King Kyŏngdŏk, began the construction of Pulguksa Temple in the tenth year of T'ien-pao (751). Taesŏng passed away during the reign of King Hyegong on the second day of the twelfth month in the ninth year of Tali (774). The nation thus had to finish the temple. Initially, the illustrious Yogacara monk Hangma was invited to stay at the temple, which has continued to exist to the present day." I do not know which of these two accounts is correct.

Who is Kim Taesŏng, the central figure of these legends? The answer to this question came from Professor Yi Kibaek. In his 1974 work *Studies on Shilla's Political and Social History*,[2] Yi claims that in *Historical Records of the Three Kingdoms*[3] Kim Munnyang occupied the post of chief minister (*chungshi*) and died in 711, while a person by the name of Kim Taejŏng is said to have served six years as chief minister, leaving the post in 750. Thus, Kim Munnyang and Kim Taesŏng, both mentioned in the *Memorabilia of the Three Kingdoms*, were most likely the same persons mentioned in the legends. The difference in the names can be attributed to the lack of standardization when rendering native Korean names into Chinese characters. The legends suggest that Kim was a child of a poor home and was raised by a renowned family that included a premier. Kim Taesŏng himself also became a premier and in the year after he left office, construction was started on Pulguksa and Sŏkpulsa temples. Twenty-four years later, Kim died without seeing the completion of these projects, which were later finished by his successors.

THE ORIGIN OF SŎKPULSA TEMPLE'S STONE GROTTO

Although Sŏkpul Temple is now known as Sŏkkuram (Stone Grotto Hermitage), it is actually a cave-temple. Called *chaitya*, such temples were first created in India over two millenia ago by cutting caverns out of rock. In India, these artificial caves were then used for religious purposes (meditation, etc.). Generally, the entrance consisted of a rectangular passageway, whereas the main hall was dome shaped. Within the main hall stood a stupa, which the worshippers circumambulated. Sŏkpulsa Temple's stone grotto was also built according to this basic structure.

In Buddhism, statues came into use around the time of Christ. At first, statues were enshrined in the main hall of stone caves. This innovation spread, leading to many famous works such as India's Ajanta caves and China's Tunhuang, Yungang and Longmen caves. In Korea, however, it was difficult to construct a cave temple since most of the country's mountains consist of old formations of hard granite. Unlike India and China, Korea does not have any of the soft sandstone which is so easily carved out. For this reason, Koreans had to modify the traditional stone cave. Examples include rock carvings such as the Paekche Buddha in relief in Sŏsan, small shrines cut from rock such as the Shilla niche Buddhas, and natural caves used as shrines such the Buddha-triad at Kunwi.

Unlike these earlier Korean adaptations, Sŏkpulsa Temple was created from an artificial cave in a style that has no precedent throughout the

A MODEL OF THE CEILING AND THE "FOREARM STONES"
The grotto was based on exquisite dynamics which utilized "forearm stones." (Model at the Shilla History and Science Museum)

world. Like early stone grottoes, the Sŏkpulsa Temple cave has a circular dome. The construction of such a dome using separate slabs of stone without mortar is no easy task. If one makes even the slightest error when fixing the dynamic tension between the slabs, the whole structure comes crashing down.

Looking at the cave, we can get a glimpse of the superb artistry and confidence of Unified Shilla craftsmen. These stone workers had already constructed Ch'ŏmsŏngdae, Sŏkpinggo and Pulguksa Temple's stonework. While constructing stone-chamber tombs, they had created stone roofs (although these were not dome-shaped). In the end, it was their expertise along with Unified Shilla's cultural exuberance that made the artificial cave at Sŏkpulsa Temple possible.

Yet, the creation of a dome-shaped ceiling was an innovation that had not been attempted before. To achieve this, Kim Taesŏng employed support stones known as 'forearm stones'. The spherical section making up the cave's dome consists of five levels. Looking up at the ceiling from the inside, one sees the first and second levels made up of twelve and thirteen concave slabs respectively. The third, fourth and fifth levels each consist of ten flat slabs. Between each of these, there are slightly projecting support blocks. These produce a 'rivet effect' which helps keep the larger slabs in place.

Dr. Nam Chŏnu came up with the apt term 'forearm stones' to describe these blocks which do in fact resemble a forearm with a bent wrist. Approximately 2 meters in length, these have been inserted vertically at regular intervals around the top of the dome. By applying pressure, they help to maintain the dynamic stasis between the concave slabs. The structure of these 'forearm stones' can best be seen on the dissected model at the Shilla History and Science Museum in Kyŏngju. The model testifies to the amazing skill of Unified Shilla artisans in general, and stone workers in particular.

THE THREE CRACKS IN THE CEILING'S COVER-STONE

Great artifacts generally have some small imperfection accompanied by an explanatory legend. In the case of Sŏkpulsa Temple's stone grotto, three small cracks can be seen in the ceiling's cover-stone. In the *Memorabilia of the Three Kingdoms*, these cracks are explained as follows:

> When Taesŏng was shaping a slab for use as the ceiling's cover-stone, the rock suddenly broke into three pieces. Taesŏng was so furious that he could hardly sleep the next night. When he finally got to sleep, a celestial deity descended and put the three fragments in place on the ceiling. When he awoke and saw what had happened, Taesŏng rushed to the southern ridge and burnt an incense offering to the deity. After this, the hill came to be known as Hyang-nyŏng (Incense Ridge).

The peak to the south of Sŏkpulsa Temple is still sometimes called Hyang-nyŏng. Yet, some claim that the original Hyang-nyŏng is actually where the parking lot now sits.

The placement of the ceiling cover-stone represents the conclusion of the cave's construction. The downward pressure of its weight establishes the dynamic symmetry of each stone making up the dome. The cover stone is 2.5 meters in diameter and 1 meter high. Its lower section has been carved to fit snugly into the cavity while the upper section (3 meters in diameter) is larger to prevent it from falling through.

As if such a technical feat were not enough, two layers of lovely lotus petals have been carved into the stone. Looking up at the ceiling of the grotto, one thus sees a blooming lotus instead of a mere stone plugging up the central cavity. The lotus, situated above the head of the main Buddha figure, almost appears to shed a soft light. The Japanese surveyor Yoneda thought of this as the sun, while Ko Yusŏp considered it to be a displaced halo.

This 20-ton stone block fell and broke into three pieces. Kim Taesŏng must have been terribly disappointed. Iryŏn, in the *Memorabilia of the Three Kingdoms*, says that Kim was "angry and grief-stricken". What could be done? In this distressed state, Kim went to sleep. The legend tells us that while he slept, he dreamed that a celestial deity came and put the three pieces into their places in the ceiling.

Legends are always based on fact. For that matter, even dreams are related to reality. For this reason, some have interpreted the legend to mean that Kim, after receiving a revelation from a celestial deity, went on to finish the project. This would imply that the ceiling cover stone originally consisted of three parts. However, this does not make sense. If Kim personally finished this massive project, which took over 20 years to complete, would he use a broken stone as its final piece?

My own interpretation is that the builders completed the project themselves while Kim was 'sleeping'. After placing 20 perimeter stones

around the cavity, they put the three pieces into place. After much long and tedious work, they were probably in a hurry to finish. They could not face carving another 2.5×3×1-meter, 20-ton stone with lotus designs. Then as now, workers tend to become impatient at the end of a project. Imagine a stone worker who had begun the project at 25 and worked on it until he was 50. If the stone broke during winter, the mood would have been especially bleak. These stubborn stone workers, who quickly completed the project anyway they could, were symbolized by the 'celestial deity' in Kim's dream.

Some time back, I spent a one-year sabbatical in America. The nights in this foreign land were often lonely. I would often lie down with the TV on, trying to forget my solitude. One night, my wife, whom I so longed to see, appeared to me in a dream. Overjoyed, I ran up to her. Waving towards me, she offered to sing me my favorite tune. In a melancholy voice, she sang the ballad *Solbat Sairo Kangmurŭn Hŭrŭgo* (Through the Pine Forest, a River Flows). This very delightful tune was from 20 years ago when I was a college student! I was so startled to hear it again, that I woke up to realize that a Joan Baez recital was playing on TV. I think that Kim's dream of a celestial deity was basically this sort of dream.

An incomplete legend always has a certain beauty to it. The fact that it is unfinished makes it that much more mysterious. Leonardo da Vinci's *Mona Lisa* has a mysterious effect since it is actually 5 percent unfinished. Likewise, the three cracks in the ceiling cover are a beautiful wound poignantly expressing the difficulties of construction.

SŎKPULSA TEMPLE IS GRADUALLY FORGOTTEN

There are no records whatsoever concerning the history of Sŏkpulsa Temple's stone grotto after Kim Taesŏng founded it. No further mention is made until 500 years later during the Koryŏ period. At this time, Iryŏn, in his work *Memorabilia of the Three Kingdoms* mentions the foundation legend and the broken ceiling cover stone.

After this, historical records fall silent for another 400 years—nearly a millennium after the grotto's construction. During the reign of the Chosŏn King Sukchong, it is finally mentioned in a travelogue. Discovered by Min Yŏnggyu, the travelogue is known as the *Mountain Diary*.[4] Written by Chŏng Shihan (styled Udam), this work is one of the rare Chosŏn-era accounts of a pilgrimage to ancient temples. If I ever get the chance, I'd love to take a field trip along the author's route. On the 15th day of the fifth lunar month in 1688, Chŏng arrived at Sŏkpulsa Temple. He has a good description of the grotto as it used to look, so I have quoted it in its entirety below.

> I talked with Kukhaeng, the monk in charge of affairs at Pulguksa Temple. After dinner, they brought me honey-water, taffy and dried persimmons, so I sat down for a while longer. Eventually, the monk who was to guide me came and we left for Sŏkkuram [meaning the hermitage at the site].
>
> We went up the rugged and steep peak behind the temple where we climbed upward for a distance of ten *li* (about 393 meters) and

then descended for one *li*. When we finally arrived, Myŏnghae from the hermitage greeted us. We sat down for a while, then went up to the stone grotto. There are Buddhist carvings at the entrance—four on one side and five on the other. They are so skillfully carved that they seem to have been created by Heaven itself. The stone gate consists of a stone piece shaped like a rainbow. Inside, there is a large stone Buddha. This majestic figure almost seems to be alive. The base is straight and exquisite. The ceiling stones and other stonework are rounded and stand straight so that there isn't the slightest leaning. The lines of Buddha statues seem to be alive. These extraordinary and incredible figures are beyond description. Such an amazing works are rarely seen. After taking an extensive look around, I went back down to the hermitage.

From Chŏng's account, we can reconstruct the current appearance of the site. At that time, the wooden antechamber did not exist. Along both sides of the passageway, there were the Eight Vajra Protectors, one of which was broken. Above the entrance where the Four Heavenly Kings stood, there was a stone piece in the shape of an arch. On the day after his visit, Chŏng met a Buddhist couple who had come from Chŏnju in order to worship at Pulguksa Temple and the stone grotto. Thus, we know that visitors and pilgrims continued to frequent Sŏkkuram.

In the 18th century, mountain temples throughout Korea were restored. Records indicate that Sŏkpulsa Temple also underwent restoration at this time. According to the *Record of Ancient and Current Construction at Pulguksa Temple*,[5] "In 1703, Chongyŏl rebuilt Sŏkkuram (the monastic quarters) and constructed a stone staircase in front of the grotto." However, there is no mention of any damage. According to the later work "Important Figures in the Restoration of Sŏkkuram"[6] by Son Yŏnggi, the stone grotto underwent a major restoration led by a Provisional Military Inspector surnamed Cho. In Son's work, the exact details and scope of the restoration aren't mentioned, but the grotto is referred to as "Pulguk's Stone Grotto", indicating that it was already a branch of Pulguksa Temple by this time.

The Sŏkkuram Buddha is thus only briefly mentioned by three or four Chosŏn literati on sightseeing trips. The paucity of records hardly does justice to such a grand monument. Yet, the most dreadful insult was yet to come as Korea became a colony of Japan.

RESIDENT-GENERAL SONE'S PLUNDERING

Around 1907, the nearly forgotten stone grotto at Sŏkpulsa Temple was reintroduced to the outside world.

A few years earlier, threats from the Japanese military had led to the Protectorate Treaty of 1905. After this time, the Chosŏn Residency-General was set up as a "protectorate government" at Mt. Namsan in Seoul, at the site of the present Agency for National Security Planning (National Intelligence Service). Ito Hirobumi was first appointed to head the Japanese colonial administration. I will have more to say about this later, but Ito was one of the leading forces behind Japan's grave robbing in Korea. He gave countless pieces of Korean celadon to the Japanese emperor and to aristocrats. Through his efforts, numerous Koryŏ tombs were also destroyed.

As anti-Japanese 'Righteous Armies' became active in the mountains, many monks fled, leaving the temples empty. Grave robbers and fortune hunters seized this opportunity to loot and destroy cultural treasures at the monasteries. At the same time, there was little awareness of cultural treasures and their value, so priceless artifacts were often sold for paltry sums.

Located high on Mt. T'ohamsan, Sŏkpulsa Temple's stone grotto went unnoticed until quite late. In a sense, this was a blessing in disguise. In August 1902, Sekino Tei, an assistant professor at Tokyo Imperial University, conducted a survey of ancient architecture in Korea. He had

THE GROTTO AS IT WAS DISCOVERED AROUND 1907 The grotto's antechamber is an open area lacking a wooden structure, and a part of the front of the dome has fallen down. Some scholars believe that a window used to exist in this part of the dome.

nominally come at the request of the Korean government. In fact, his visit following the Sino-Japanese War of 1894, was a part of an extensive land survey, in preparation for the colonialization of Korea. Sekino saw the dilapidated Pulguksa Temple at this time, but was not even aware of Sŏkkuram's existence. Likewise, the official Japanese historian Imanishi conducted a field trip to Pulguksa Temple in 1906, but did not find out about the stone grotto.

By 1907, there was talk of "a giant stone Buddha buried on the east side of Mt. T'ohamsan" in Japan. This somewhat exaggerated rumor began with a mailman who happened to discover the site and reported it to the postmaster (who was Japanese). As the rumor spread, thieves finally made their way to this steep and rugged mountain. They took two statues (probably the most beautiful ones from the original ten) from the grotto's ten niches. Difficulty in transporting such heavy stone carvings probably prevented them from taking more.

Thinking that there might be a relic hidden underneath the Buddha, the thieves even took a chisel and broke off some stone at the base of the figure. During restoration work, the broken shards were recovered and reapplied, but the 'scar' still remains. Of the original 40 Buddha, Bodhisattva and tutelary figures, 38 now remain. Shortly after this incident, three of the four lion figures were stolen from in front of Pulguksa Temple's stupa. All three were in excellent condition.

In the autumn of 1909, Sone Arasuke, who had assumed Ito's position as Residency-General, came to Kyŏngju with his entourage on his first round of inspection. Like his predecessor, Sone stole a tremendous number of cultural treasures. He was mainly interested in Buddhist art and old books. In his brief tour of less than a year, he seized huge piles of old manuscripts from old residences, temples and Confucian academies. These works were donated to the Japanese emperor and thus ended up in the palace library. Officially known as the 'Texts Donated by Sone Arasuke,' these were some of the cultural treasures eventually returned to Korea in 1965 as a result of the Korea-Japan Peace Accord.

In spite of his august position, Sone made the difficult climb up Mt. T'ohamsan to Sŏkpulsa Temple. After the dignitary paid his visit, the beautiful marble pagoda that stood in front of the Eleven-Headed Avalokitesvara statue suddenly vanished without a trace. Sone clearly ordered his men to take it. Since the stone grotto was originally based on the Indian *chaitya*, there were probably small pagodas both behind and in front of the main Buddha statue. The former was apparently taken by Sone while the latter was destroyed (the pieces are on display at the Kyŏngju Museum). At present, all that remains at the grotto are two pagoda bases in front of the Dharma Protector statues. The cube-shaped bases have a square cavity on top where the sarira were originally enshrined.

Yanagi Muneyoshi has quoted oral reports about Sone's looting and the lost statues, but it is even more striking to hear such things from two colonial administrators. The first one, Moroga, was commissioned as curator of the Kyŏngju Museum. In his pamphlet, "Shilla Relics of Kyŏngju",[7] he reports the following.

According to oral reports, Buddhist sarira were enshrined within a small marble pagoda that stood in front of Sŏkkuram's Nine-Headed [Eleven-headed] Avalokitesvara statue. In year 41 of the Meiji era [should be autumn of year 42, or 1909], a noble and high official came on a tour of inspection after which the pagoda disappeared without a trace. Even now, this saddens me to no end.

The other testimony comes from Kimura, who came to Korea when the Residency-General was first established. Working as Chief Scribe, Kimura served as guide during Sone's visit to Sŏkkuram. In his 1924 work "Growing Old in Korea",[8] we find the following:

Priceless objects such as the two stone grotto Buddha statues, the pair of lions from the Pulguksa Temple stupa and the stone lantern [sarira pagoda] were sold by thieves and transported to Japan. My one wish before dying is to see them returned so that the central shrine is once more complete.

This is the definitive evidence provided by the Japanese themselves that the Resident-General Sone was responsible for the theft. When reading these Japanese accounts, I'm especially touched by the words "this saddens me to no end" and "my one wish before dying." These writers were, after all, Japanese themselves. Should we then assume that their sentiments are false or hypocritical? I don't think so. On the other hand, I don't believe they said this out of sympathy for Korea, as Yanagi did. Their feelings simply exhibit their sense of responsibility as Japanese public servants. As officials in charge of colonial possessions, they felt that they had failed to fulfill their duty. This sense of dominion was a significant force behind that occupation, and in a sense, was far more terrifying than plundering and theft.

THE FINIAL AND SUPPORT STONES
FROM THE BROKEN PAGODA
*There were two marble
pagodas in the grotto.
The intact pagoda was
stolen by Resident - General
Sone while fragments from
the broken pagoda were
placed in Kyŏngju National
Museum. Only a support
stone with an empty
reliquary space remains in
the grotto.*

After visiting Sŏkpulsa Temple's grotto and making off with the small pagoda, Sone went back to Seoul and sent the art historian Sekino to the site. After hearing Sekino's report, which praised the cultural artifacts as "unparalleled throughout East Asia," Sone considered measures for the restoration and preservation of the grotto. He finally drew up a plan for moving all of the grotto's statues to Seoul. The plan entailed dismantling the grotto, transporting the stone pieces to Kamp'o on the east coast and then shipping them to the port of Inch'ŏn. The Residency-General immediately ordered the Kyŏngsang Province Governor to notify the County Magistrate of the plan and have him draw up an estimate of the cost. However, the plan was rash under the current circumstances. According to Kimura's "Growing Old in Korea", public opinion was also cool to the idea. When Sone finished his tour of duty, the plan was therefore scrapped. Hence, with the formal annexation of Korea, Sŏkkuram's fate was thrust into the hands of Terauchi.

GOVERNOR-GENERAL TERAUCHI'S RESTORATION

In 1910, Japan formally annexed Korea. Terauchi, the first Governor-General, ran the military government responsible for colonial administration and management of national assets. Land surveys were also conducted as a part of the colonial government's plan to gain complete control over the country's cultural assets. Under Sekino Tei, a survey of old Korean texts was also performed. A mere glance at the survey's annual reports and yearly *Index of Ancient Korean Works*[9] shows how zealously the work was carried out. Japan had gone from plunderer of cultural treasures to custodian. In short, this meant that colonial assets were now viewed as belonging to the Japanese government.

The Governor-General made an on-site survey of important relics at Sŏkkuram and the rest of the Kyŏngju area. Its June 25, 1912, report reads as follows:

THE GROTTO BEING DISMANTLED
On June 15, 1914, the entire grotto, except for the main Buddha figure and the ceiling cover stone, was taken apart. Imprisoned by wooden scaffolding, the Buddha wears a troubled expression.

One could say that its [Sŏkkuram's] extraordinary structure and exquisite carvings make it the foremost artifact from its era. About a third of the dome-shaped ceiling has fallen in, leaving a hole. Dirt and sand from the mountain thus falls through the hole onto the statues. If left as is, the remaining two-thirds of the ceiling will collapse, damaging the figures on the central wall and destroying the large statue of Sakyamuni. An East Asian art work of unparalleled excellence would thus be obliterated.

After this assessment, Terauchi personally made a field trip to the grotto on Mt. T'ohamsan and gave instructions on the restoration work to be done. Kuniji, from the government's Office of Civil Engineering, was dispatched to the site to draw up plans for the restoration. His report, dated April 8, 1913, reads as follows:

...first of all, the stonework must be dismantled. The surrounding stone walls must be reconstructed and reinforced with concrete with a uniform thickness of 3 *cha* [1 meter]. As far as possible, original stones should be used for the ceiling, with additions made only where necessary. Above the ceiling, a concrete reinforcement of 3 *cha* should be used to keep it from falling. There was originally a ceiling over the front entrance, but it was destroyed during the Middle Ages. If this area were covered with reinforced concrete, it would be highly effective in preserving the stone images. When the estimated cost for the project is calculated, it roughly comes to the sum listed in the supplement.

Following this report, a blueprint and budget were written up and on September 12, the Office of Civil Engineering submitted its plan to the Ministry of Home Affairs. On the following day, Sekino Tei added his assessment of the project, which was then sanctioned by Governor-General Terauchi.

DISMANTLEMENT OF THE GROTTO

Sŏkpulsa Temple's grotto was thus dismantled for the first time since its creation. In October 1913, wooden scaffolding was put in place to hold the ceiling stones while the structure was disassembled. With the scaffolding completed in December, a wire fence was erected around the grotto to keep people out during the winter. On May 21, 1914, the work recommenced and by June 15, the roof had been completely taken down. The interior carvings were removed by August 17 and the dismantling work was completed on September 12 (according to a report by the on-site foreman, Ishijima).

From September 27, the excavation work was begun for the concrete reinforcement and, on October 9, workmen started pouring the concrete. While doing this, the workers discovered two springs coming from the stone wall in the back of the grotto. These had originally flowed underneath the cave's stone floor, reappearing in a stone water-fountain in the chamber. The workmen, unable to understand this sophisticated system (later explained by Dr. Yi Taenyŏng), used zinc pipes to drain the water to the outside.

Looking at the list of workers at the 1914 dismantlement, we discover that the stone masons and carpenters were all Japanese. Koreans were only employed as general laborers. In contrast with the stone masons, who earned 2 won and 10 *chŏn* per day, the Koreans received only 45 *chŏn* per day. On the other hand, Japanese doing the same work received 1 won.

The concrete consisted of one part cement and one part sand to four parts gravel. The mortar between the stones consisted of a hard mixture of one part cement to one part sand.

The grotto After dismantlement
By September 12, 1914, the grotto had been completely dismantled. Here, the Ten Disciple carvings are seen leaning against a wall.

In May 1915, the reconstruction began. The grotto's external wall originally consisted of a 1.65-meter-thick "double wall of jade and polished stone" which surrounded the inner wall. This allowed for sufficient ventilation. Japanese technology, or to be more precise, modern technology, was unable to replicate this. Hence, a 1 meter wall of stacked stone was used along with a support panel. This was reinforced by a 2-meter-thick external wall of concrete. The use of cement in the repair work made long-term preservation of the cave impossible. Cement emits carbon dioxide gas and calcium—elements that damage stone monuments. Unfortunately, the Japanese only thought of cement's usefulness as mortar and thus generously applied it when repairing important monuments such as Sŏkkuram, the Punhwangsa Temple Pagoda and the Miruksa Temple Site's pagoda. At Sŏkkuram, the cement was especially damaging since it prevented ventilation. The completion ceremony for these calamitous repairs was held on September 13, 1915. The project had taken three years to complete and had cost 22,726 won.

According to Nam Chŏnu's analysis, the repair work could have been limited to the forward ceiling section. This large project, involving complete dismantlement, the construction of a 2-meter-thick wall and the substitution of 286 stone blocks, is thought to have been Terauchi's scheme. In a sense, he was saying, "You uncivilized Koreans aren't able to properly take care of a single monument. Under the protecting hand of the Japanese Empire, the monument has been repaired using the most modern techniques and materials. This demonstrates what can be done now that Japan has annexed Korea!"

Instead of a minor restoration, the Japanese undertook a major reconstruction which permanently damaged the monument. Numerous changes were also made to the exterior. Yanagi Muneyoshi, in his article "Concerning Sŏkpulsa Temple's Sculptures"[10] in the June 1919 issue of Art,[11] puts forth the following criticism.

When I saw this [the reconstructed stone wall], I was amazed by the lack of taste. It could now be mistaken for the entrance to a tunnel. What were the builders thinking? I don't think of their work as 'repair,' but as new vandalism. The engineer might claim that a scientific restoration had been undertaken, but it seems to me that he failed to understand the meaning of artistic restoration...If I only could, I would like to tear down the stone wall, and have the Koreans themselves do the repairs...Sŏkpulsa Temple was fortunate to avoid the wrath of Japanese pirates, but it has now suffered a new disgrace under the name of 'restoration'. ...One wonders how beautiful the grotto would have been had the builders simply fixed the roof and put the stone wall back in its original form. When I look at old pictures of the grotto when it was in disrepair and pictures taken after the restoration, I cannot help but feel disgust at these wicked, scientific workers that seem to know nothing of art.

Endless Humidity and Moss

As mentioned above, the materials and methods used in the restoration detracted significantly from the grotto's aesthetic charm. Yet a more severe problem was leakage. In 1917, just two years after the restoration was completed, drainage pipes had to be installed on the outside of the dome to prevent rain water from seeping in.

Even after this, the leakage continued. Thus, a third restoration had to be undertaken from 1920 to 1923. At this time, waterproof asphalt was rubbed over the concrete reinforcement on the ceiling. Since the zinc pipes were unable to handle all the water from the springs, a conduit was constructed to drain the water out the structure's right side. One can get an idea of the scale of this project from the fact that it cost 16,980 won—70 percent more than during the first restoration.

In spite of the costly third restoration, the grotto's moisture problems

were not solved. Green moss damage was visible throughout the monument. In 1927, the Governor-General tried to find a way to wash the moss off using steam. To this end, a boiler was built and installed. Thus in the end, the moisture problem could not be solved through restoration, but had to be treated by means of a mechanical device instead .

The steam cleaning eroded the grotto's stone work, causing permanent damage. Even the Japanese seem to have been aware that there were problems with this method, but there was little else for the Japanese government to do. The steam cleaning method used at this time did not resemble a gentle sauna. To the contrary, it involved spraying the structure with scorching steam from a shower nozzle. A locomotive engineer was called from Kyŏngju Station and, after the boiler was fired up, the structure was sprayed with scalding steam. Since even the force of water drops can erode a stone structure, it doesn't take a scientist to imagine what spraying steam from a hose would do.

In 1927, the steam cleaning managed to wash off all the green moss, but with the passing of time, it grew back. On August 16, 1933, the governor of North Kyongsang Province presented the chief of the Office of Education with the following report.

Previously, there was some green moss, but this has now multiplied due to the heavy monsoon this summer. The cave is full of moisture and drops are continuously falling from the ceiling...If left the way it is, there is a danger of erosion. An expert in these matters should therefore be dispatched...to offer recommendations.

Thus, in 1934, the dreadful boiler was started up again and the grotto was given another steamy baptism.

After liberation from Japanese rule on August 15, 1945, the Korean people inherited the Sŏkkuram problem. During 36 years of occupation, all the Japanese had to show for their efforts was a 2-meter-thick concrete wall, incessant moisture and moss, and a steam cleaner. These became a part of the grotto's ignoble legacy.

1. *Samguk yusa.*
2. *Shilla chŏngch'i sahoesa yŏn'gu* (Seoul: Ilchogak, 1974).
3. *Samguk sagi.*
4. *Sanjung ilgi.*
5. *Pulguksa Kogŭm ch'anggi.*
6. *Sŏkkuram Chungsu sangdong mun.*
7, 8, 9, 10, 11. Translation of original Japanese title.

Pursuing the Mysteries of Sŏkkuram

Pak Chonghong / Yanagi / Ko Yusŏp / Yoneda / Yi T'aenyong / Nam Ch'ŏnu /
Kim Iksu / Kang Ubang

PAK CHONGHONG'S FRUSTRATION

At the same time that the Japanese colonial administration's technicians were defacing the Sŏkpulsa Temple grotto, other scholars were zealously attempting to understand the monument's beauty and mystery. The first researcher to take up this task was a 19-year-old Korean by the name of Pak Chonghong (1903-1976). Young people today no longer even know Pak's name. If it were mentioned that he drew up the National Charter of Education, some might remember him, but it isn't his later deeds that I want to focus on here.

Pak was a leading Korean philosopher and one of the greatest Korean thinkers of the twentieth century. Back when I was preparing for the college entrance exam, his writings were frequently on Korean tests. Actually, it was at this time that I first read his works. When I entered the university, I even had the opportunity to take his popular introductory course on philosophy. I can still vividly recall his talks on themes such as the future direction for Korean scholarship and issues facing the Korean intellectual.

In his youth, the philosopher Pak had dreamed of becoming a student of art history. In his writing "Personal Reflections: Prior to My Pursuit of

Philosophy",[1] he vividly describes how he had a fool-hearted desire to write the history of Korean art at the young age of 19.

Pak says that he most of all wanted to compose a work that would explain the unique character of the Korean people. By doing so, he hoped to rekindle Korean pride, which had suffered so much during the Japanese occupation. While a history of Korean thought would have been an ideal way to bring out the uniqueness and greatness of the Korean spirit, Pak knew that he was not up to such a grand endeavor. He also considered a history of Korean music, but realized that his knowledge was too meager. He therefore began reading all the books he could find on aesthetics and art history. Filled with a sense of mission, he started writing a history of Korean art. The work eventually appeared as the "Unfinished Manuscript on Korean Art History"[2] published serially in 12 consecutive issues of the magazine *Kaebyŏk* beginning in April 1921. It was also published in the first chapter of the *Complete Edition of Pak Chonghong's Works*.[3] In this work, Pak covers the period from the ancient past before coming to an abrupt stop at the Three Kingdoms period. As implied by the article's title in *Kaebyŏk*, it is incomplete. The reason for this is to be found at the Sŏkpulsa Temple grotto. Pak, a teacher by this time, went up to Mt. T'ohamsan during his summer break as a part of his research on Unified Shilla art. He describes his experience at the site.

> One year, I stuck Lipse's aesthetics book in a trunk and went to Kyŏngju's Sŏkkuram. There, I spent the summer in a tiny hermitage in front of the grotto. I intended to explain Sŏkkuram according to Lipse's theory of sculpture. I virtually lived inside the cave at this time; yet I could not figure out how best to proceed. After spending much time there, I could tell that the lighting was different in the morning and evening. When the sun rose, the grotto looked nice, but when the Sakyamuni statue was illuminated by the full moon, the whole place became a realm of mystery. Realizing my inability to explain

THE EAST SEA AS SEEN FROM THE GROTTO I would often climb Mt. T'ohamsan in the autumn in order to see the sun rise against the East Sea, on the horizon.

Sŏkkuram, I completely lost my determination to study art history. I strongly felt that I must resume my studies at a more fundamental level.

At this point, Pak Chonghong gave up his study of Korean art history. In the following year, he entered the university, where he resumed his studies beginning with an introduction to philosophy. Later, when he came across Yanagi's writings on Sŏkpulsa Temple, he was deeply impressed. At this time, he stated that his choice to abandon art history had been for the best.

The first person to write a full description of Sŏkpulsa Temple's beauty was Yanagi Muneyoshi (1889-1961). In an addendum to his article "Regarding the Sculptures at Sŏkpulsa Temple"[4] that appeared in the June 1919 issue of *Art*[5] he writes:

> For a long time now, I have had a special fondness for Korean art...During my travels, the sculptures at Sŏkpulsa Temple were particularly unforgettable and thought-provoking. It seemed to me a pity that this world masterpiece was still not widely known among the general population. I thus became the first person to introduce this work to the public extensively.

> It saddens me that I have written an extremely dull description for the sake of objectivity...but I still feel that I have been able to convey

THE GROTTO WHEN THE ANTECHAMBER WAS OPEN
In this picture from a souvenir sold during the Japanese occupation era, one can clearly see the antechamber in which the last guardian figures are facing inward.

my love of this site and I believe that my understanding of the site is at least partly correct.

Yanagi's lovely prose style is indeed absent in this writing. I suppose this is unavoidable. After all, this text is largely made up of quotes from the *Memorabilia of the Three Kingdoms*[6] and the *Records of Pulguksa Temple*[7] and includes diagrams of 40 carvings. There are even individual descriptions for each statue. Nevertheless, when he describes the artifacts at the site, he becomes ecstatic.

Truly, Sŏkkuram expresses the unified plan of a single mind. Unlike India's Ajanta caves or China's Longmen Grotto, the cave is not a conglomeration of accumulated sculptures. Throughout this tranquil composition, one finds one mind. It is an indivisible, organic whole in which none of its part detracts from one another. In both external and psychological terms, it is a complete unity of amazing thoroughness and detail.

Walking into the cave, one's mind also enters an inner world. The magnificent Buddha quietly and silently maintains his unmoving composure as he sits upon a lotus pedestal. Looking up at the image, one cannot help but be impressed by its grandeur and beauty. This is entirely an inner, spiritual realm. With four female Bodhisattvas in front of him, the Eleven-Headed Avalokitesvara behind and his beloved Ten Disciples to his left and right, he pronounces the glory of eternity. The figures within the hall seem to be praising his joyous Dharma. This is not a realm of external force, but rather a realm of inner depth. It is a realization of beauty and peace. Its spiritual energy is grand and profound. What a clear contrast between the inside and outside of the cave! All things seem to be drawn inside. Power is transformed into depth. Things live in stillness instead of movement.

The whole significance of religion seems to be present within Sŏkkuram.

In his explanation, Yanagi continually praises the grotto. However, his words are much more than a mere list of superlatives. They convey deep reflections on the cave's psychological, philosophical and religious significance.

Yanagi says that he had no formal training in art history. Even so, he had the discernment to notice the transformation from the dynamic guardian figures on the outside of the cave to the inner, contemplative realm as symbolized by the Buddhas and Bodhisattvas inside. Moreover, he said he felt a gradual development in both style and content. He compared this to the ceiling of the Sistine Chapel where one can trace Michaelangelo's subtle development over a five-year course from his first work (*Noah's Ark*) to his final work (*Creation*).

Yanagi made another keen observation concerning the figures' lines of vision. He discusses the psychological transformations of a single devotee who circles the hall paying homage to the figures. He explains this in terms of the statues' lines of vision. He goes on to discuss why the Eleven-Headed Avalokitesvara and Dharma Protector figures, which are carved of single stone blocks, are in high-relief while the other relief figures are in bas-relief.

In every respect, Yanagi was an outstanding art historian and an expert at analyzing designs and motifs. His eulogy on Sŏkpulsa Temple is at its best when he describes the central Buddha figure.

Could anyone fully explain the significance of this sculpture? Its beauty is to be found in the fact that it defies explanation. On the other hand, it does not strike one as technically elaborate...It lacks exaggeration or complexity. In this supremely simple work, the sculptor clearly portrays the supreme dignity of the Buddha. Its entire

THE TEN DISCIPLE FIGURES These representations of the Buddha's ten chief disciples each has a distinct expression and are all turned in the direction that the devotee is to walk when paying respect to the Buddha.

significance is to be found in its elegant countenance. Its mouth is closed in silence while its eyes seem to be resting. Within the dark calm of the grotto, it sits absorbed in meditation. This is the silence which speaks of all things....the stage of nothingness which embraces all things. Whatever may be true or beautiful can never surpass this....here, religion and art are one.

Yanagi's observations and introspective reflections on Sŏkkuram come from a perspective different from that of scholastic research, which is based on aesthetic observations. For this reason, many people consider him to be an essayist or an author of *belles-lettres*. But I would disagree. Looking at a silent object, Yanagi is able to describe the empathy that it arouses. This requires more than mere writing skills. Yanagi insists that he is not a scholar of aesthetics, but when he says that he places more importance on "the method of doing philosophy" than on "the study of philosophy", he demonstrates a deep insight into the methodology of aesthetics.

In his work *Korea and Its Art*,[8] Yanagi praises the Korean aesthetic, which he describes as tragic beauty. He says that Korean art employs lines as a way of portraying sorrow. From a nationalist standpoint, this view of Korea must be overcome. I would also have to reject Yanagi's commiserating attitude. From a cool, objective, academic standpoint, much criticism has been leveled at Yanagi's subjective and exaggerated feelings, and in the academic world, he is not respected. Even so, I respect the man. Who has loved Korean art as much as he? Everyday I feel I have something to learn from his compassionate and respectful attitude.

THE CLASSICAL ART THEORY OF KO YUSŎP

As Yanagi himself pointed out, his work was the first explanation of the grotto. It was Ko Yusŏp (1905-1944, styled Uhyŏn) who went on to conduct a comprehensive and definitive study of the site from the standpoint of Korean art and cultural history.

Considered the father of Korean art history, Ko wrote a number of important treatises, including "Shilla Art Handicrafts",[9] "Our Art and Handicrafts",[10] and "Kim Taesŏng". In these writings, he gives the Sŏkpulsa Temple grotto his highest praise while analyzing its design and interpreting its spiritual history.

Ko begins his research with a description of his respect, and love for pride in the grotto. The following excerpt is from his writing "Our Art and Handicrafts", which was written in the 1930s.

The giant lotus pedestal is beautiful, but the dignified Buddha who sits upon it is truly grand. Approximately 3 meters tall, the Buddha's hands are in the 'Conquering Demons, Touching the Earth' mudra. His gentle yet dignified phoenix-eyes are only half open. Sitting in the Lotus Posture, the Buddha's upturned foot seems relaxed and tranquil while his knees are gently rounded. The plump, elongated hands look soft and gentle while the shoulders and arms provide a sense of harmony. Sitting with back straight, his chest projects forth in a noble fashion. The earlobes extend downward, the lips are thick and the ridge of the nose is high. His pupils and hair are exquisite also.

This great statue, beginning as a bloodless, passionless lump of granite, has been endowed with a strong pulse, breath, divinity, gentleness and dignity. When unveiled, the joy was surely not limited to the sculptor, but extended throughout Shilla and echoed throughout the cosmos.

Ko describes the cave's structure as vibrant. He goes on to describe how the halo fits in perfectly with the structures on the back wall of the grotto and the lotus design on the ceiling cover stone.

Statues often have a nimbus, which can include a halo (*tugwang*) and the aura (*shin'gwang*) around the Buddha's body. Normally, a nimbus is placed directly behind the Buddha as a part of the statue. For this reason, it often looks rigid and unnatural. This Buddha's halo, situated on the wall far away from the statue, has avoided these faults. Even more importantly, it seems to move freely in accordance with the perspective of the observer. When the observer finally comes

THE MAIN BUDDHA FIGURE AND THE UNATTACHED HALO The separation of the Buddha figure and his halo is the most exquisite feature of the grotto's overall structure. This innovation eliminates the halo's decorative function and gives the statue a sense of dynamic motion instead.

in front of the Buddha statue and looks up into its friendly face, the halo suddenly appears as a lotus behind the figure. This is the reason for the lotus flower design on the ceiling. Although the lotus is spatially distant from the figure, it is always highlighting it from above. This unique feature is seen on no other Buddha sculptures. When viewed objectively, most sculptures suffer from a sense of rigidness due to the fact that they are separate works carved from stone. We can only marvel at the Sŏkkuram Buddha, which has completely avoided this rigid feeling in favor of a fluid and natural realism.

Classics are Classics Everywhere

Ko classifies Korean sculpture into three general trends. Those of the Three Kingdoms period are characterized by symbolism, those of the Unified Shilla period by classicism or even idealism and those of the Koryŏ period by romanticism.

Buddha statues from the Three Kingdoms period focus exclusively on the front view, completely ignoring how the statue appears from the side. Without any variation in the flesh and muscles, the statues look like so many assembled parts. The folds in the robes are completely stylized, leaving an overall impression of mechanical rigidity and a symbolism of abstract mystery. Unified Shilla statues, on the other hand, have fleshy, voluminous figures. They have a more developed sense of depth and appear larger, with each curve in the body preserving the organic connection between each part. The statue lacks explanatory or superficial elements. With a totally idealized composition, it still maintains an authentic realism. In this way, sculptors of the Unified Shilla period portrayed an abstract mysticism via concrete sensory elements. Ko therefore felt that the Sŏkkuram Buddha was an idealist work standing at the pinnacle of classicism.

Kim Wonyong (styled Sambul) later adopted this classification in its original form in his theory of art history.

The Sŏkkuram sculptures are works demonstrating the acme of mid-eighth-century carving. As a synthesis of external and internal beauty, these works may be called the height of religious sculpture. One feels that they represent the sculpturing techniques amassed and cultivated for 200 years since the sixth century. The melancholy expression, the quiet smile: such gestures from the past are sublated. From this point on, Shilla Buddha statues calmly sit in a deep silence.

The smile has disappeared from their lips, never to be seen again. With the passing of the ages, their expression gradually becomes more rigid and frightening. The faces become expressionless and eventually devolve into a cold stereotype. The Sŏkkuram images stand on this precipes before the fall.[11]

A Buddha statue is an image of absolute being, produced by man. God, the absolute, or perfection, appears in a human form, as the ideal image of man. This is the harmonious, ideal beauty that all ancient people sought after.

When an ideal order has been achieved through the transcendence of all opposites, such art is valued as 'classical'. Moreover, any classical art agrees with all other classical works. This is true regardless of spatial divisions like East and West or chronological divisions such as ancient and modern. With this in mind, Ko, in his writing "What Can We Learn From Ancient Art?",[12] interprets the art of Sŏkpulsa Temple's stone grotto from an international perspective.

In his critique of Greek art, Wilhelm Winkelmann said that it possessed "a noble simplicity and quiet grandeur". Clarity and vibrance as seen in the depiction of nudes are considered to be Apollonian qualities, while the stylistic synthesis of sensitivity and intelligence is described, by Hegel, as the classical aspect of Greek art. All these qualities can also be attributed to the grotto.

YONEDA'S SURVEY OF THE GROTTO

Sŏkpulsa Temple's stone grotto is described as a religious and scientific masterpiece. Yanagi and Ko Yusŏp were responsible for explaining the cave's artistic value, but a detailed explanation of its scientific value had to wait for the civil engineer Yoneda Miyoji.

Yoneda graduated from the architecture department of a Japanese technical school in 1932. In the following year, he accepted an invitation (in spite of the low salary) to do work for the Museum of the Government-General of Korea. Once in Korea, Yoneda devoted himself to surveying old buildings. As an assistant of Fujita, he did survey work when Sŏkpulsa Temple was being repaired. Later, he conducted surveys of the pagoda at Chŏngun-dong's Sach'ŏnwangsa Temple in Kyŏngju, the Chŏngam Village temple site in P'yŏngyang, the Chŏngnimsa Temple site in Puyŏ, as well as Pulguksa Temple and Sŏkkuram. While surveying Paekche's Puso Fortress, he came down with typhoid fever and died on October 24, 1942, at the young age of 35 (he was unmarried).

However, Yoneda presented a number of papers three years before his death. With titles such as "The Proportions of the Tabo Pagoda", "The Decorative Scheme of the Five-story Pagoda at the Chŏngnimsa Temple Site", "The Construction Scheme of Pulguksa Temple" and "Astrological Thought Appearing in Early Chosŏn Architecture", Yoneda's landmark works clarified the mathematical relationships within Korea's classical architecture. After his death, Yoneda's manuscripts were compiled and published in a work that was to become a classic in the study of Korean architectural history. (The original work, written in Japanese and published in 1944, was later translated by Shin Yŏnghun and published under the title *Studies on Early Chosŏn Architecture*.[13])

His paper "The Construction Scheme of Grotto in Kyŏngju", which was included in this book, provided an essential clue to understanding the scientific puzzle of the grotto.

Yoneda's investigations into Sŏkkuram's construction plan began with an inquiry into the length of the *cha*—a unit of measurement used during the Unified Shilla period. Scholars had previously assumed that the *cha* in use at the time was equivalent to a *kokch'ŏk* (30.3 cm). In his survey of the Pulguksa and Sŏkpulsa temples, Yoneda discovered that this assumption was incorrect. Measuring each part of the temples' stone stupas, he kept coming up with measurements equal to 0.98 *kokch'ŏk*,

1.96 *kokch'ŏk*, 23.6 *kokch'ŏk*, etc. He therefore concluded that the *cha* used by Unified Shilla stone masons was equal to 0.98 *kokchŏk* (29.7 cm)—a unit of measure that he dubbed a *tangch'ŏk*.[14] He rounded these off to 0.98 *kokch'ŏk*. When examining these detailed measurements, one cannot help but be impressed by the precision achieved by the ancient stone masons. To ensure that his survey was accurate to the last detail, Yoneda even made a metal ruler that had the same length as that used by the original Unified Shilla stone masons.

Yoneda's survey showed that the grotto's rotunda had a radius of 12 *cha*. If a hexagon were inserted into the circular chamber, the entranceway, also 12 *cha* in length, would have been equivalent to one side. The Buddha statue actually stands slightly back from the center of the chamber. If one imagines the entranceway, 12 *cha* across, as one side of an equilateral triangle, the front of the Buddha pedestal would touch the tip of the triangle.

The antechamber was slightly altered when it was repaired in 1960. The last guardian figures on each side had originally been turned perpendicular to the other figures, but during this restoration, these were set back in line with the other figures. However, when Yoneda did his survey, the length from the entrance of the antechamber to the point where it met the base-line of the above equilateral triangle was three times the distance from the base-line to the front of the Buddha pedestal. In order to clarify these observations, Yoneda drew up a 3-*cha* (about 1 meter) long blueprint, explaining the intricate relationships among the different parts of the cave.

Looking at the cave's vertical scheme, the carvings on the main wall along with their pedestals stand 12 *cha* in height. The height of the shrine enclosure is 12 times the square root of 2, the square root of 2 being the length of a diagonal line across a square. The area from the shrine enclosure's ceiling to the grotto ceiling forms a semi-circle with a 12-*cha* radius. The height of the main Buddha figure and pedestal together come to 12 times the square root of 2 *cha*.

The pedestal consists of two lotus petals with a *kansŏk* (support stone), in the form of an equilateral octagon, between them. The *kansŏk* is 5.2 cha, while the diameter of its base is 5.2 *cha* (one-half the height of an equilateral triangle measuring 12 *cha* on each side, and the length of a diagonal across a square measuring 5.2 *cha* on each side). The pedestal's lower support stone is equivalent to a circle inside an equilateral octagon measuring 5.2 *cha* on each side.

In this way, Yoneda explained the proportional relationships of the grotto's construction. He demonstrated that the structure was based on a measurement of 12 *cha*, and that squares and their diagonals (the square root of 2) were used, along with the height of equilateral triangles and the perimeter of circles enclosed within hexagons and octagons.

The Buddha image is 11.53 *cha* high. The knee span is 8.8 *cha*, while the shoulder span is 6.6 *cha*, chest width 4.4 *cha* and the face width 2.2 *cha*. If the 8.8-*cha* knee-span is taken as the base of an equilateral triangle, the point of the triangle touches the Buddha's chin.

Although he lacked experience as a surveyor, Yoneda was able to make a precise and comprehensive analysis of the mathematical relationships of the grotto's sculptures, including calculations of the basic unit of measurement down to the fifth decimal as 0.98207 *kokch'ŏk*. This attention to minute detail opened up the cosmic dimensions of the grotto's design. Based on the figures from his survey, Yoneda wrote a short treatise called "Personal Reflections on the Sŏkkuram Grotto's Expression of the Cosmos". In this work, Yoneda refers to the astronomic mathematics that formed the basis for Mesopotamia's astronomic calendar. Although his idea is highly speculative, I quote a short portion below.

The grotto's design is based on a circle (with 360 degrees corresponding to the 360 days of the year) with a 12-*cha* radius (and thus a 24-*cha* diameter, which corresponds to the 24 hours in a day). The 12-*cha* entrance corresponds to the 12 hours that traditionally make up a day in Northeast Asia. The dome (the universe) was constructed with the same circular shape as an expression of the realm of eternity. The center (the ceiling cover-stone) is in the shape of a circle (sun) and is decorated with a huge lotus. Between each flat stone of the sphere, elbow stones poke through, evidently as a representation of the stars.

Yoneda lived a short life, but one full of meaning. Up until his early death at the age of 35, this young, greenhorn technician worked under the glaring sun, surveying ancient fortresses and other sites. This previously unknown student of architecture devoted seven years of his life to making surveys of painstaking precision. Based on his research, he was able to arrive at the above conclusions after just three years of work. He serves as a fine example of how to pursue an academic discipline and how to live one's life.

His life and research vividly demonstrates the 'power, greatness and beauty of the small'. When the assistants of the American architect Ludwig Mies van der Rohe brought him a large number of architectural drafts to look over, he told them to bring just one. As he explained, "Less is more." Tung Ch'i-ch'ang, a Ming Dynasty painter of the Literati School, once copied the famous paintings of former masters in a small album. He titled the album, "There are great things within the small." In his research, Yoneda practiced this methodology of finding the great in the small, and the same can be said of his life in general.

THE SHILLA PEOPLE'S SCIENCE AND TECHNOLOGY

Yoneda's precise survey and the mathematical relationships brought to light by his findings have provoked much thought and interest in Shilla science and technology. For those studying the history of Korean science, his research represents both a great achievement and avenues for further investigation.

According to Prof. Kim Yong'un, Shilla had founded an educational institution for mathematics which was primarily devoted to finance and accounting. However, this institute did not teach geometry in the Western sense of the term. If we look at Sŏkkuram, we find that a knowledge of geometry was used in a number of ways, which can be classified as follows:[15]

1. Establishment of a basic unit of measurement.

2. Division of this unit into equal parts.

3. Use of the square and its diagonal (square root of two) and the use of this measurement to form three-dimensional models.

4. Use of proportional numbers to determine the design of the main Buddha figure.

5. Use of equilateral triangles and partition of its vertical line.

6. Use of a single side of an equilateral hexagon and a circle adjacent to its external perimeter.

7. Use of an octagon and an internal circle.

8. Use of circles and the circular constant (the ratio of the circumference of a circle to its diameter).

9. Use of spherical surfaces.

10. Use of ovals.

Dr. Nam Ch'ŏnu (formerly professor of physics at Seoul National University) adamantly opposed the restoration of the grotto that took place in the 1960s. He claimed that, as we researched the grotto's structure, we would become more and more aware of its awesome mathematical harmony. In the May issue of *Shindonga*, he described its technical mystery as follows:

The grotto's main hall was geometrically constructed with an amazing degree of accuracy. This degree of accuracy reaches 1,000 to 1, or even 10,000 to 1. If we consider that 10,000 to 1 means a 1-millimeter discrepancy per 10 meters, we get a sense of how accurately each of the grotto's stones was placed.

Moreover, the grotto's main room is perfectly circular, with fifteen carvings demarcating the circle. Looking at this, one cannot help but be amazed at the way the Shilla people freely worked with large blocks of granite as if they were dough. One likewise feels a sense of awe at their knowledge of geometry that formed the basis for such an undertaking.

The Shilla people's mathematical skills were astounding. They found the hexagram within the circle of the main hall and then used one side of this hexagram for the entrance. They were able to accurately divide arcs and precisely divide the ceiling's dome into ten parts. Dr. Nam Chŏnu continues:

> The Shilla people knew *pi*, the circular constant, to a much greater degree of accuracy than 3.141592. They probably had, at the very least, a geometry that included the sine principle of dodecahedrons; that is to say, the accurate sine value of 9 degrees.

REASON FOR THE SPRING UNDER THE GROTTO

Across from Sŏkpulsa Temple's stone grotto, there is an open area, on the other side of which a natural spring flows out of a large rock slab. Strangely enough, this spring (referred to simply as *kamnosu* or 'sweet dew water') turns into two springs which flow under the stone wall of the grotto. When the grotto was restored in 1913, the Japanese tore away the natural stone in order to lay a concrete wall. At this time, they discovered the spring passing underneath. In order to prevent moisture damage, they installed zinc drainage pipes.

When the grotto was again restored in 1963, this spring water once more presented a difficult problem. The zinc pipes had rusted through and thus had to be replaced with copper drainage pipes.

During the Japanese occupation and the Third Republic, moisture in the cave was primarily attributed to the spring which produced a strong flow of a liter per every ten seconds.

In 1961, Dr. H. Planderleith, the head of the UNESCO World Heritage Center, was invited to Korea for the grotto's restoration. Planderleith mentions the drainage problem in his first report.

Yi T'aenyŏng (former Seoul National University chemistry professor) was one of the first people to express skepticism about previous research into the problem.

Dr. Planderleith said that 2-meter pipes should be installed to deal with the spring water. I put forward the following questions and proposal. "If the water really flowed up into the cave and made everything wet, why did the Shilla people build the grotto on top of the spring? What's your opinion on this? Don't we need to find out how this cave, which has existed for well over a millennium could have been preserved?" I proposed the following experimental method as a hypothesis. Even if my hypothesis is wrong, it should be of value in research on the original structure. While I cannot confidently declare that zero percent of the spring water made it up into the cave, almost all of the water seems to be from condensation...In this case, it is important to measure the temperature of both the caves surfaces and air, so that we may understand the differences in airflow in the morning and evening as well as in summer and winter...I proposed that particular emphasis be put on the relationship between humidity and temperature. Dr. Planderleith accepted my proposal and created a second report according to these corrections.

However, those who carried out the restoration did not accept Dr. Planderleith's second report.

Looking at the debate over this issue, I discovered something very interesting and important. Scientists like Dr. Yi T'aenyŏng and Nam Ch'ŏnu had faith in the Shilla people's scientific outlook. It must be noted that unlike the mechanistic science of the 20th century, Shilla's sophisticated science utilized natural principles. For this reason, scientists tend to agree that the only way to solve the problems of Sŏkkuram is to restore it to its original form.

However, art historians, archaeologists and administrators, i.e., those who don't fully understand science, felt that some technique or device of modern science could surely save the grotto.

Why did Kim Taesŏng create the grotto above a spring? Since many spots on Mt. T'ohamsan look over the East Sea, why was this site chosen? Dr. Yi T'aenyŏng is to be credited with solving this mystery. During a history conference in February 1973, he presented his paper "Sŏkkuram's Structure and the Moisture Problem".[16] The paper's essential argument was presented in the magazine *Pŏpshi* as in the following excerpt:

> The condensation on the rock surfaces of Sŏkkuram results from the fact that the temperatures on the stone surfaces are out of balance. Before the restoration by the Japanese colonial government [i.e., when Sŏkkuram was in its original state], the temperature of the grotto's floor was lower than that of the walls where the stone carvings were, due to the two springs that ran under the grotto. As a result, condensation only occurred on the floor, and this was the only part of the cave that suffered from erosion. However, during the two restorations undertaken by the Japanese, the floor was reinforced with quicklime while pipes were used to drain off the springs. In addition, concrete was poured into the area behind the ceiling's cover

stone. Consequently, the stone floor, which should be cold, became warmer, while the area around the ceiling cover stone became cooler. This led to water forming on the exquisite sculptures along the walls.

So this was the problem. The Shilla people were aware that a mere temperature difference of 0.1 degree Celsius would cause water drops to form on the colder side of an object. They wisely placed the stone floor above springs in order to maintain a temperature between 4 and 10 degrees Celsius. In this way, all the condensation would occur on the floor, leaving the rest of the grotto undamaged.

In conclusion, the moisture problem could be completely solved with the removal of the concrete wall from the Japanese colonial era, the wooden antechamber, the glass barrier from the Third Republic era and drainage pipes.

This goes to show that the true scientist is someone who follows natural principles rather than one who opposes them.

THE SUN RISES IN THE EAST

Situated at 565 meters above sea-level on the eastern face of Mt. T'oham, Sŏkpulsa Temple's grotto faces 30 degrees east-southeast. It thus looks out at the remote East Sea horizon. For years, the structure's orientation was a mystery. Why is it turned 30 degrees to the south instead of facing directly eastward? The Japanese assumed that the site had been chosen simply for convenience's sake.

In the 1960s, Dr. Hwang Suyŏng, the general supervisor for the grotto's restoration, presented a paper stating that the grotto was facing the East Sea port where King Munmu's Taewang'am was located. Many people still believe this to be correct. In support of this theory, Dr. Hwang in 1967 even claimed that Taewang'am was an underwater grave and the grotto's main figure was that of Amitabha Buddha.

Dr. Hwang points out that stone Buddha statues were often placed near royal tombs during the Shilla period. He therefore concluded that Sŏkkuram was a Buddha overlooking King Munmu's Tomb. This theory accords well with the idea that Taewangam and the Sŏkpulsa Temple grotto were a part of 'national protection' Buddhism, that the grotto was built to protect the nation from Japanese invasions and was related to prayers for the true-bone Kim clan's safety. The theory also agrees with the legend that Kim Taesŏng built the temple for his parents in his previous life.

However, there are a number of problems. Sŏkpulsa Temple was constructed during King Kyŏngdŏk's reign. During the 71 years that had passed since King Munmu, other kings (i.e., Kings Shinmun, Hyoso, Sŏngdŏk and Hyosŏng) had successively occupied the throne. Moreover, the exact position of Taewangam, when seen from the grotto, is too far left (east). One still might conclude that the grotto faces Taewangam since the rock lies in the general direction; however, this does not accord well with the awesome scientific precision evident in every aspect of the grotto's construction.

The theory that Sŏkkuram faces Taewangam also receives insufficient support from the legends of Kim Taesŏng or King Munmu. It also makes little sense from a Buddhist standpoint. While it is generally agreed that *hoguk* (national protection) Buddhism was powerful around the time of the Three Kingdoms' unification, it is hard to believe that the massive Sŏkkuram project was undertaken 100 years later, during Shilla's heyday, in order to glorify the nation's military culture. Just as I believe that the existence of an underwater tomb at Taewangam is an unconfirmed conjecture, I do not think that the builders of the grotto designed it to face Taewangam. A scholar can put forth a theory according to his or her own subjective views, but such views must survive the scrutiny of disciples and readers. During the period of military dictatorship, blind patriotism supported an irrational attitude that led to distortions of the truth. The manufactured history of great historical figures was a part of

THE GROTTO'S ORIENTATION *This picture was taken by Dr. Nam Ch'ŏnu, who proved that the grotto did not face Taewang'am but actually faced 30 degrees southeast, the direction of the sunrise during the winter solstice.*

Labels in image: Estuary on the East Sea ▼ | Taewang'am ▼ | 30 degrees southeast The direction that the cave face ▼

this legacy. This nationalist propaganda was, in the end, just as harmful as the Japanese propaganda that had preceded it. A theory might seem patriotic and wonderful, but if it is not grounded in truth, it ultimately leaves nothing to the world but lies.

Dr. Kim Wonyong also rejected the idea that the positioning of the grotto was "to protect the nation". On the contrary, he felt that its orientation was due to a spiritual ideal. When debate over the issue was raging in 1969, Dr. Nam Chŏnu asserted that it was by no means a trivial issue. In his article "The Sophisticated Shilla Science Forgotten at Sŏkkuram,"[17] Doctor Nam claimed that Sŏkkuram did not face Taewang'am at 28.5 degrees but, instead, faced the point where the sun rises during the winter solstice (29.4 degrees).

We must keep in mind that the grotto originally did not have a wooden antechamber but was, instead, an open structure. The sunrise during the winter solstice would thus be seen from the grotto. To ancient people, the solstice did not signify the end, but rather the beginning, of the year. If the mathematical relationships of the grotto's structure are taken into account, the orientation towards the winter solstice make perfect sense.

For us nowadays, 'the sun rises in the east' is a fact we take for granted—which goes to show how alienated we have become from nature. In this respect, ancient people seem to have been much more scientific and philosophical than us moderns. The new year now begins on January 1st—a date with no significance or relation to natural events. The solstice, on the other hand, signified that exact point when the *yin* forces finally entered decline, leading to the rise of *yang*.

WAS KIM TAESŎNG 170 CENTIMETERS TALL?

There are around 350 books and theses written about the Sŏkpulsa Temple grotto. A few more, and they'll have to make a new academic discipline called 'grotto-ology'. Authors of these works include researchers in a wide range of fields including art history, archaeology, history, Buddhology, architect, history of science, natural science and preservation science. One of the more interesting works on the cave was written by Kim Iksu, a sculptor and professor at Youngnam University. His treatise "Views Concerning the Original Layout of Sŏkkuram"

("Sŏkkuram wonhyŏng'e kwanhan kyŏnhae") was published in 1980 in the 14th edition of the *Youngnam University Thesis Collection.*[18]

Kim agreed with Nam Ch'ŏnu's theory that the grotto was originally open and the last two guardian figures in the antechamber were not turned inward towards the entrance . He also put forth the interesting theory that Kim Taesŏng was 170 centimeters tall.

Kim looked at the grotto from a sculptor's perspective. He knew that once the size of the Buddha images was determined, the sculptors would have had to decide on the height of the pedestal and the ideal distance from which to view the figure.

While doing a survey of the grotto, Kim discovered that the halo on the back wall was actually oval instead of round. From left to right, it measures 224.2 cm across, compared to 228.2 cm from top to bottom. This is to compensate for the optical illusion that occurs when looking at a circle from an angle. In normal circumstances, the circle would seem to bulge at the sides, but the extra 4 cm makes it look perfectly round when seen from a particular vantage point.

Where is this point? According to modern design principles, the best place from which to view an object is a distance three times the maximum height (or length) of the object. With framed paintings, it is three times the length of a diagonal across the frame. According to this principle, the observer's line of sight to the top and bottom of the object would form a 20-degree angle.

For the Sŏkkuram Buddha, the ideal angle would therefore be in the middle of the antechamber. Seen from this point, the Buddha's face could appear above, within or below the halo, depending on the observer's height. Kim made exact calculations based on his findings and concluded that a person's eyes would have to be 160 cm from the ground for the head to appear in the center of the halo. It is interesting to note that this happens to be the exact height of the pedestal. If the person's eyes were 160 cm from ground level, he would have stood 172 cm tall; and if the height of the person's straw shoes (2 cm) is taken into account, the leader of the project (Kim Taesŏng) would have been 170 cm tall.

WHO IS THE CENTRAL BUDDHA FIGURE?

The central statue at the Sŏkpulsa Temple grotto is commonly referred to simply as the main Buddha figure. This is because there are different opinions, some claiming that it is Sakyamuni, while others say that it is Amitabha or Vairocana. The Buddha's hands are definitely in the 'Conquering Demons, Touching the Earth' mudra. When the Buddha attained enlightenment, he completely conquered all the demons who had tried to tempt him. He then touched the Earth, calling on it to confirm his enlightenment. In this mudra, the forefinger of the right hand is slightly raised. The mudra thus lends support to the theory that this is a Sakyamuni statue. Min Yŏnggyu, a proponent of this theory, points out that the symbolism of the Tabo and Sŏkka Pagodas at nearby Pulguksa Temple is derived from the "Looking at Jeweled Pagodas" section of the *Lotus Sutra*. He therefore concludes that the grotto's statue represents Sakyamuni Buddha giving a sermon on Vulture Peak. Prof. Mun Myŏngdae, on the other hand, believes that it is a Sakyamuni figure from the "Kwanfo sanmei ching".

Dr. Hwang Suyŏng, on the other hand, claims that it is an Amitabha figure. As can be seen in the Kunwi Buddha Triad, Amitabha figures from the Unified Shilla period can also appear in the 'Conquering Demons, Touching the Earth' mudra. The Amitabha faith is known to have been widespread during the mid-eighth century. The Eleven-Headed Avalokitesvara statue behind the main figure and the 'Sugwangjŏn' (Longevity Brilliance Hall) signboard, which hung on Sŏkpul Temple during the 19th century, also support this theory.

Others claim that the figure represents Vairocana—the Buddha symbolizing the Buddha Dharma itself. Prof. Kim Rina points out that the Buddha appearing in the 'World Lord's Wondrous Dignity' chapter of the

Flower Garland Sutra manifests his body in the 'Touching the Earth' mudra even when he appears in other places and guises. As Vairocana, this Buddha appears accompanied by Sakyamuni's retinue.

Amid this debate, Kang Ubang discovered an important fact which is beyond dispute. To begin with, Kang believed that any research on the Buddha should begin with the Japanese surveyor Yoneda's treatise. However, Yoneda only discussed the grotto's structure. He never explained why the measurements of the main Buddha figure (the most important element of the grotto) were 11.5 *cha* in height, 8.8 *cha* across the knees and 6.6 *cha* across the shoulders.

Kang searched through numerous texts trying to find what these numbers were based on. When reading Hsüan-tsang's famous account of his travels to India, he happened to come across the same numbers. Hsüan-tsang (600-664), a monk during China's T'ang Dynasty, describes the erecting of a figure depicting Sakyamuni's enlightenment at Mahabodhi Temple in India's Buddha Gaya.

> Entering the monastery, I saw a Buddha statue. With a dignified posture, it was seated in the lotus posture. Its right foot was on top, while its left hand was placed above its lap and its right hand was hanging down [in the Conquering Demons mudra]. The figure sat facing the east. Its solemn expression made one feel that the Buddha was truly present.
>
> The pedestal was 4.2 *cha* high and 12.5 *cha* wide. The statue was 11.5 *cha* high and measured 8.8 *cha* across the knees and 6.2 *cha* across the shoulders. The facial expression was of one who had perfectly fulfilled all vows. Its compassionate expression seemed like that of a living person... Everyone wanted to know what sort of person had created this work.

Except for a 0.4 *cha* difference in shoulder width, the statue's proportions and orientation are the same as those of the Sŏkkuram Buddha. The Sŏkkuram statue is clearly modeled after the Sakyamuni figure from Mahabodhi Temple in Buddha Gaya.

Kang claims that this does not necessarily mean that the Sŏkkuram figure is only Sakyamuni. Since Vairocana and Sakyamuni are seen by some sects as essentially equivalent, the figure may therefore represent both Sakyamuni and Vairocana.

Throughout the years, Buddhist scholars and art historians conducting research on the grotto's iconography have typically perused sutras and treatises in search of doctrinal support for their theories. However, Buddhist statues do not directly reflect the history of doctrine. To the contrary, iconography is more closely connected with the religious faith of a particular era. Thus, the layout of the 40 figures enshrined in the grotto may actually be based on quite simple principles. One can safely assume that the figures around the central Buddha statue represent the Shilla people's most familiar and cherished Bodhisattvas, devas, Arahants, etc., in an arrangement reflecting their respective roles. In my opinion, the central figure represents the general ideal of an enlightened being (a 'Buddha') and does not signify any Buddha from a particular scripture.

MASTER HALF-STEP

Early in the summer of 1986, when Yi Yonghŭi was serving as chairman of the Daewoo Foundation, I had the opportunity to take part in a joint expedition. The research team had chosen to focus on stylistic changes in the royal tombs of Shilla. As a 'bonus', the group went to the Sŏkpulsa Temple grotto with Chŏng Yangmo (head curator of the Kyŏngju Museum) as its personal guide. After spending an hour at the site, everyone went to dinner.

At this time, Kang Ubang, who had just returned from his studies in America, presented a short paper on the direction of research concerning the grotto. He announced for the first time that he had discovered the exact same proportions while reading Hsuan-tsang's travelogue. Tongju, one of the academics in the group, was amazed and overjoyed at hearing this.

"That is a great discovery! Congratulations!"

"Yoneda's rediscovery of the length of the Shilla *cha* was what made it possible. In terms of Yoneda's research, I have now taken merely half a step forward."

"Half-step! Mr. Kang, from now on, you should take on the penname Panbo (Half-step). That has a nice ring to it. It'll be even better when you are older and people start calling you Master Panbo."

Master Panbo's efforts and achievements are to be found in his ability to take a minor point and manifest its full significance. I really envied him on that day.

1. Toksŏ hoesang—naega chŏrhagŭl kuhagikkaji.
2. "Chosŏn misulsa mijŏnggo".
3. *Pak Chonghong chŏnjip* (Seoul: Hyŏngsŏl Ch'ulp'ansa, 1982).
4, 5. Translation of original Japanese title.
6. *Samguk yusa.*
7. *Pulguksa sajŏk.*
8. Translation of original Japanese title.
9. "Shillaŭi misul kongye".
10. "Uriŭi misulgwa kongye".
11. Kim Wonyong and An Hwijun, *Han'guk misulsa* (Seoul: Seoul National University Press, 1993).
12. "Urinŭn kodae misulesŏ muŏsŭl paeul kŏsin'ga".
13 *Chosŏn sangdae kŏnch'uk ŭi yŏn'gu* (Seoul: Han'guk Munhwasa, 1976).
14. To be exact, Yoneda's survey concluded that the *cha* used at Pulguksa Temple was 0.980125 *kokch'ŏk* while that of Sŏkkuram was 0.98207 *kokch'ŏk.*
15. This is taken from *Iyagi kwahaksa.*
16. "Sŏkkuram-ŭi kujowa sŭpki munje".
17. "Sŏkkuramesŏ manggakdoen kodoŭi shilla kwahak", *Chindan hakpo*, No. 32, 1969.
18. *Yŏngnam taehakkyo nonmunjip.*

Even Inanimate Objects Have Life

The 1963 Restoration / The Antechamber Problem /
The Dome Window Issue / Preservation Problems / Shilla History and
Science Museum / Yu Ch'ihwan's Poem / Sŏ Chŏngju's Poem

FIRING UP THE OLD BOILER

In November 1946, one year after liberation from Japanese rule, the terrible boiler left by the Japanese was fired up once more and the grotto was given a steam cleaning. Unable to eliminate the causes of moisture in the cave, there was perhaps little else that could be done. In 1953, just after the Korean War, the boiler was used again. However, this time, the cleaning was carefully done by workers from the Kyŏngju Museum. The third cleaning following Liberation was undertaken in 1957. This time, the work was entrusted to the Kyŏngju Educational Board's janitorial service. These workers, in a hurry to finish the cleaning before a group of foreign tourists visited the site, ignored regulations concerning the temperature of the steam and the distance requirement (a foot). Newspapers soon reported that the grotto was being washed with burning steam and stiff brushes. When the government got wind of this, the vice minister of Education was sent to the site to ascertain the actual situation. As a result of this incident, the Office of Cultural Properties, which was then under the Ministry of Education then, established the Investigative Committee for Restoration of Sŏkkuram in January 1958. During Syngman Rhee's term in office, three research teams were sent to inspect the site.

*ELEVEN-HEADED
AVALOKITESVARA
In higher relief than
the other figures, this
'Goddess of Mercy'
statue has a 6.5 ratio
between face and
body, proportions
which give the figure
a this-worldly beauty.
Perhaps this was
modeled on "Miss
Unified Shilla".*

The Sŏkkuram restoration project was stepped up after the fall of Syngman Rhee in 1960. On May 21, 1960, Pae Kihyŏng was asked to draw up plans for the work and on March 16 of the following year, the Committee of Cultural Properties reviewed Pae's blueprints for a double dome.

On May 24, in the aftermath of the *coup d'etat* of May 16, 1961, the Committee of Cultural Properties convened and unexpectedly rejected Pae's plan. On June 7 of the same year, the architect Kim Chungŏp was asked to come up with a new plan. This sudden change in planners set the project back to square one. Concerning these changes, the official report only says, "These changes were measures...reflecting trends following the Military Revolution of May 16."

PARK CHUNG-HEE'S RISE TO POWER AND THE PROGRESS OF THE CONSTRUCTION PROJECT

While the restoration stalled due to the sudden change of designers, Dr. Planderleith (head of the UNESCO World Heritage Center), who had been invited a little earlier, visited Korea. He arrived on July 17, 1961, and inspected Sŏkkuram on the 21st. He concluded that the earth covering the grotto had to be removed in order to see what was causing the moisture and drainage problems. The Ministry of Education quickly called together a meeting and approved his plans. The work to remove the soil commenced on July 31. This was in preparation for the actual restoration work, which was to take place in 1964.

The project had been put on hold for three years. It is sad to think that there was no restoration plan at the time; yet the Ministry of Education felt compelled to call an urgent meeting to approve the recommendation of a single foreign scholar.

As mentioned earlier, a renewed impetus for the restoration project came following the *coup d'etat* by Park Chung-hee. Before long, Park Chung-hee had completely seized power, and in the so-called

Revitalizing reforms in October (allowing him more than two terms in office), he altered the Constitution so that he could remain in power for life. (One could even say he succeeded since he stayed in power until his death by an assassin's bullet on October 26, 1979.)

In support of his dictatorship, Park fully used the symbolism of cultural treasures. Indeed, he had been interested in historical artifacts from early on. Projects directly undertaken under the direction of 'His Excellency' include the restoration of Pulguksa Temple, the construction of Hyŏnch'ung Memorial Shrine in Asan, the excavation of Ch'onmach'ong, the 'Five Thousand Years of Korean Art' exhibition and plans for moving the Haeinsa Temple Sutra Repository. During these projects, Park would typically give his personal instructions concerning each detail. The generic, pale-yellow, concrete houses that we now see next to cultural treasures were originally Park's idea. In the end, his excessive interest and interference in the 1960s restoration of Sŏkkuram caused the grotto to suffer yet another disgrace. We can now look back with regret at the period's events, but at the time, the project was pursued with zeal as an expression of the dictator's strong convictions.

PLANDERLEITH'S SECOND REPORT

The restoration work was divided into survey, preparatory work and main construction. In order to ensure smooth progress, two central supervisors were appointed: Hwang Suyŏng from the Committee of Cultural Properties and the architect Kim Chung'ŏp.

The basic aim of the project was to eliminate whatever was causing the moisture and moss. In particular, the plan called for (1) a double dome to prevent water from flowing in; (2) fortification of the drainage pipes for the springs under the floor to keep ground water from seeping in; (3) a wooden antechamber to prevent moist air from entering the structure; and (4) underground conduits connected to the space between the two domes in order to promote ventilation within the structure.

A DISSECTED MODEL OF THE CONCRETE DOUBLE DOME
The basic plan for the 1963 restoration called for a second concrete dome to prevent leakage. This model was created by the Shilla History and Science Museum.

The basic assumption behind the plan was that the moisture problem was due to an influx of moist air. However, Dr. Nam Chŏnu, one of the most devoted researchers on the grotto, had already pointed out that the grotto's moisture problem was not due to water leakage, but rather to condensation. In other words, dew was forming as a result of the sharp temperature difference between the inside and outside, and this eventually formed into drops of water. Unlike the construction plans, which sought to prevent air from getting in, the grotto needed to be open (i.e., restored to its original form) so that air could move around freely. Unfortunately, Doctor Nam was not commissioned by the Committee of Cultural Properties at this time; hence his words fell on deaf ears.

On July 21, Planderleith arrived in Kyŏngju. After a one-day inspection of the site, he submitted a statement saying that the construction team's plan was sound. With this statement, the decision was final, and the preliminary work of removing the soil covering the grotto thus began on July 31.

Planderleith was a world-recognized authority on the scientific preservation of cultural treasures. After submitting his initial report, he continued to make inspections of the site. He also exchanged opinions with natural scientists like Dr. Yi T'aenyŏng. Through this additional research, he finally realized that there were sharp temperature differences in Korea's seasons (ranging from 35 degrees Celsius in the summer to -15 degrees in the winter), not to mention condensation due to the relative temperature and humidity inside and outside the structure. He therefore revised his conclusions, which he put forth in a second report. Submitted on August 18, the report represented the results of 25 days of research.

> According to my survey, the area is both hot and humid, with daytime temperatures reaching 35 degrees Celsius and humidity 95 percent in August. On nights when the temperature falls to 30 degrees, dew forms on the cold surfaces. For this reason, the most important measure to prevent moisture would be ventilation: blocking off the grotto would be a huge mistake. Hence, I cannot but help correct my previous assessment. After giving it much thought, I must say that I am all against placing a roof over the entrance or adding a door to the structure.[1]

However, Planderleith's second report was ignored. The construction team's plan had become fixed.

When I read this, I see two aspects of Planderleith's personality. On the one hand, he was proud or careless when, in a display of his authority, he submitted his initial report after a single day, claiming that his inspection was complete. On the other hand, 25 days after his work was done, he took it upon himself to submit a second report, which was not required. In this sense, he demonstrated the conscience of a true scholar.

The Stone Grotto Becomes a Wooden Grotto

The wooden antechamber in front of the grotto was constructed to prevent the influx of moist air; yet this was not the only reason that it had been planned. According to the construction team, an antechamber had been part of the original grotto. During previous excavations around the grotto, a roof tile bearing the inscription 'Sŏkpulsa Temple' had been discovered. However, it was not clear whether this was a tile from a wooden building or whether it had been used to keep water from seeping through the cracks in the roof cover stone.

In support of the theory that a wooden structure previously existed at the site, Dr. Hwang Suyŏng and the construction team pointed out that such a building was depicted in the painting *Kolgul Sŏkkul* (Bone and Stone Grotto) by Chŏng Sŏn (styled Kyŏmjae). However, this work, said to have been painted in 1733 when Chŏng was 58, is not realistic—unlike other extant paintings done when Chŏng was in his sixties. Rather than attribute this inferior work to Chŏng, some scholars have even claimed that the painting was done by his grandson Chŏng Hwang. Moreover, the painting's title *Kolgul Sŏkkul* seems to refer to Kolguram (Bone Grotto Hermitage) near Kirimsa Temple.

The installation of an antechamber with a wooden roof did not preserve the grotto or help restore it to its original form. Nevertheless, the construction went on as planned, turning the *sŏkkul* (stone grotto) into a *mokkul* (wooden grotto). It was Doctor Hwang's idea to use a wooden structure for the antechamber, and President Park also seems to have favored the idea.

Debate Over the Display of Carvings in the Antechamber

On July 31, 1961, work to remove the earth covering was carried out. By September 13, a construction office was built at the site. The preparatory phase of the work lasted until June 30, 1963.

During the preliminary work, the main restoration plans continued to be discussed. At a meeting on October 18, 1962, Hwang Suyŏng and Kim Chungŏp, the two project supervisors, expressed conflicting opinions concerning the wooden building. Twelve days later, Kim was dismissed from his position and his design contract was canceled several days later. Dr. Kim Wonyong was appointed as Kim Chung'ŏp's replacement on November 13.

Hwang Suyŏng and Kim Chungŏp's differences centered around the wall of the wooden antechamber, and whether the figures should be displayed in two even rows or with the figures turned inward. At the time, the figures of the Eight Guardians were turned so that they faced outward. It was suggested that they should instead be lined up in two groups of four (a violation of the grotto's original form). Dr. Hwang Suyŏng claimed that this mistaken arrangement of all the figures in rows came from the Japanese restoration. The linear display of the Eight Guardians would also destroy the 'awesome scientific precision' evident in the grotto's geometrical proportions.

On February 16, 1963, the newly appointed supervisor Kim Wonyong inspected the stone carvings at the site and concluded that since the non-linear display was indeed the original arrangement, the figures should not be set up in lines of four. Eleven days later, ten other people involved in the project went to the site and reached the same conclusion.

On July 1, 1963, the main restoration work began and, a day later, Dr. Kim Wonyong was dismissed, leaving Hwang Suyŏng as the sole supervisor of the project.

The restoration team had to obtain permission from the Committee of Cultural Properties before it could rearrange the guardian figures. The committee, however, did not give permission, leading Hwang Suyŏng to announce his desire to resign. Despite this conflict, Hwang Suyŏng was not dismissed. He then began to dismantle the figures as a part of his 'research'.

On October 12, the Committee of Cultural Properties, after debate over

EIGHT GUARDIAN FIGURES Of the Eight Guardians on both sides of the antechamber, the two at the end are different from the others, indicating that the last figures were originally turned inward.

the issue, rejected a proposed vote and declared instead that the figures could be rearranged in two straight rows with the proviso that all objections be included in the final report.

When I first heard of this, I understood for the first time why court sessions and congressional meetings are always recorded in the minutes. People naturally want proof of their own good judgment and conscientious actions when future generations comb through such documents.

A detailed account of the project can be found in the *Report on the Restoration of Sŏkkuram.*[2] Personally, I could not understand why the committee tried to force this issue, but an explanation may be found in Nam Ch'ŏnu's work *Sŏkpulsa Temple.*[3]

This was still a period of rule by the military. Thus, it was difficult for the Committee of Cultural Properties to stand up against government pressure even to this extent. After this, the committee was weakened and devolved into an advisory organ.

On October 17, just five days after forcefully obtaining the committee's assent, Park Chung-hee and his entourage personally made an inspection of the site, providing further impetus to the work.

Park was a Seoul-based politician responsible for a revolution. Yet just five days after he heard of the decision to rearrange the Guardian figures, he arrived at Sŏkkuram on Kyŏngju's Mt. T'ohamsan. He had obviously rushed over there as fast as he could. Having stubbornly opposed Park's opinion, the committee had reversed themselves. This victory wasn't enough for Park: he wanted to personally visit the site as soon as possible.

THE WATER GROTTO, DARK GROTTO AND ELECTRIC GROTTO

On July 1, 1964, there was a completion ceremony for this restoration project, which had been pushed through in spite of the committee's objections. The work had taken three years to complete.

Needless to say, President Park Chung-hee attended the ceremony. In spite of all the work, water could be seen running down the grotto wall. After three years of work to prevent seepage and moisture, the cave was drowning in water. The mass-media took off with the story. Journalists sarcastically played with the name in their headlines: "Is it Sŏkkuram or Su [Water] guram?", "Sŏkkuram is Am [Dark] guram." There was so much moisture in summer that the main Buddha figure looked as if it were taking a shower.

The heavy seepage following the restoration was primarily due to the restoration team's misguided attempt to enclose the grotto. The double dome was an even bigger problem than the wooden antechamber. As Dr. Nam Ch'ŏnu had pointed out, the water that formed in the grotto was not due to leakage. Since the warm air that formed inside the double dome could not escape, the relative temperature and humidity within the grotto were much lower, leading to condensation. The wooden antechamber prevented warm air from entering the grotto, but did not remove the humidity from the air. Dr. Nam Ch'ŏnu explained the principle as follows.

> During the monsoon season, the air inside one's house feels much drier than the air outside. This is not because the air lacks moisture. The air inside is simply warmer, and this means that the humidity, relative to that outside, is lower.
>
> Although closets and cellars both have doors on them, no one would feel at ease if their closet was placed in their cellar during the humid summer months. This is because everyone knows that, in summer, it is always moist inside a cellar. Housewives know that leaving the door open during the day helps keep cellars a little dryer.[4]

However, a thoroughgoing investigation into the grotto's moisture problem was never undertaken. Later, people tried to eliminate the moisture via mechanical means. Two years after the restoration, Dr. Kim Hyogyŏng from Seoul National University's Engineering Department was asked to work on such a device. Eventually, an airconditioning system was installed in the cave. Thus the grotto acquired yet another nickname: Chŏn [Electric] guram. Instead of searching for thoroughgoing preservation measures, restoration teams had made a 'mokkuram' (wooden grotto) and 'amguram' (dark grotto). Since it then began to turn into a 'suguram' (water grotto), they transformed it into a 'chŏn'guram' (electric grotto). Today, after 30 years have passed, one can still hear the hum of the air conditioner running 24 hours a day, 365 days a year.

A WINDOW IN THE DOME

Park Chung-hee's concern for the grotto and other cultural treasures

may have been due to his personal disposition and interests. However, dictators generally have taken an interest in cultural relics and public works for propaganda purposes and as a way to show off their 'competence'. Governor-General Terauchi built a concrete reinforcement while Park Chung-hee had a nice wooden building built as an antechamber. Their projects may have differed, but their underlying objectives were the same.

As it became apparent that the restoration work was ineffective, Nam Ch'ŏnu wrote his article "The Crisis in Maintaining Sŏkkuram's Original Form".[5] This set off the famous 'Sŏkkuram Debate'. Following Nam's article, Shin Yŏnghun (who had been the on-site supervisor of the construction) published his article "The Sŏkkuram Restoration Did Not Make Things Worse"[6] in the July 1969 issue of *Shindonga*. This was followed by Mun Myŏngdae's article, published in the August 1969 issue of *Wolgan Chung'ang*, criticizing Doctor Nam's statement that the grotto's situation was critical. Nam Ch'ŏnu then published a follow-up article to

"The Crisis in Maintaining Sŏkkuram's Original Form" under the same title in the August issue of *Shindong'a*.

Concerning the issue of preservation, Nam Ch'ŏnu insisted that the grotto originally had an impressive open structure. He also demonstrated that there was originally a window on the front of the dome. In addition, he claimed that the ten niches in the grotto were originally not flush with the outer wall, but were set back instead so that a hidden area at the base of the niche was actually open to the outside, allowing ventilation.

During the Japanese restoration, some of the original stone pieces could not be identified. These were piled up next to the grotto. Nam, while inspecting these fragments, came across a long arch-shaped stone which he claimed was part of a window. This stone piece can now be seen on the side of the steps leading down from the grotto. Most visitors

A PART OF THE DOME WINDOW AMONG DISCARDED FRAGMENTS FROM THE ORIGINAL GROTTO
Next to the stone steps leading down from the grotto, there are fragments from the original construction. Among these, there is an arch-shaped fragment that was used for the window. Prof. Kim Iksu took this picture after carrying the separate pieces over to one spot and piecing them together.

have no idea what the stone is, and children can often be seen jumping on top of it or sitting on it.

MINUTES OF THE 1991 SPECIALIST CONFERENCE

The attempt to regulate the grotto's temperature and humidity by mechanical means led to numerous problems. For example, a breakdown—even if only temporary—caused great damage to the structure. The grotto was like a person who never leaves an airconditioned room in the summer. When the airconditioner broke down, it was covered with sweat.

Even though the visitors could ignore the incessant hum of the machinery, the constant vibrations undoubtedly had an effect on the grotto. After all, even drops of water repeatedly falling on a stone can eventually wear it away. In this sense, there is a great difference between merely maintaining a site and preserving it for posterity.

The removal of humidity by using an air conditioner was, to some extent, a success. However, the moisture problem did not disappear entirely. When Planderleith came back to Korea in 1970, he looked at the condition of the grotto and recommended that (1) the wooden antechamber be removed and (2) insulation installed in the hollow part of the dome. Needless to say, his recommendations went unheeded.

The Office of Cultural Properties assigned research of the grotto to the Korea Advanced Institute of Science and Technology with Dr. Yang Chaehyŏn as director of the project. It was concluded that the grotto was being damaged by the presence of visitors. As a result, in 1971 regular visitors were no longer allowed to go inside the glass enclosure. With this rule in effect, visitors had to peer at the Buddha from a distance greater than that allowed when visiting a convict in a prison. From this vantage point, one could not even see the shadows of the Buddha's retinue.

In 1991, the research center of Cultural Properties held the 'Conference of National Specialists on the Scientific Preservation of Sŏkkuram'. This took place at Sŏkkuram and was held for three days from December 11 to 13. Specialists attending the conference included Kim Wonyong (archaeology), Hwang Suyŏng (art history), Chang Kyŏngho and Shin Yŏnghun (architectural history). Experts in preservation and natural science included Yi T'aenyŏng (chemistry), Kim Hyogyŏng (mechanical equipment), Kim Chonghŭi (materials technology), Chŏn Sangun (history of science), Min Kyŏnghŭi (biology) and Yi Sanghŏn (geology). Kim Tonghyŏn served as chairman of this conference of leading authorities.

The conference's conclusions were summarized as follows in the minutes.

At present, the grotto's general state of preservation is good; hence fundamental changes are not required. However, a monitor should be installed inside the grotto in order to identify long-term erosion. With respect to the problem of the grotto being sealed off and the issue of lighting, the lights should be dimmer and ways should be found to have them shine upward from below. It has been decided that the noise and vibrations from the dehumidifier are not a significant problem; yet these might have a long-term effect on the grotto. For this reason, the present apparatus should be exchanged for one that makes less noise and vibrations, or the room housing the mechanism should be moved further away from the cave. Furthermore, in order to ascertain the grotto's original form and to note changes, a committee for the preservation of Sŏkkuram should be established or conferences of experts convened. An exhibition hall with a model of the grotto should also be created in order to provide education to visitors. There was general agreement that, instead of hosting international symposiums, Korean experts should be sent overseas for training.

I was able to learn a great deal whlie reading this report, which contains many allusions to the general direction of research on the grotto. Since the conference was not convened in order to review the actions of those responsible for the restoration or mechanical equipment, it is little wonder that Nam Ch'ŏnu, who had spent his life criticizing the project, was not invited. Ironically, some of the experts who attended admitted that this was their first visit to the grotto.

When I read this report, I want to ask one question to all those involved with the grotto: "Do you believe that inanimate objects have life?" I do believe that even inanimate things have life. When a rock is broken up and becomes dust, doesn't it cease to live as a rock? And yet we say that the stone carvings in the cave have somehow become weaker than the other stones lying exposed on Mt. T'ohamsan. What does this mean? It means that the stone has become diseased. Didn't the people at the conference notice that the central Buddha's right elbow is peeling as if it had some skin disease? How can one conclude that there are 'no significant problems'? Reading the minutes of the conference, my eyes caught Kim Wonyong's remarks. His sentiments reflect the direction in which preservation efforts need to be directed.

Whenever I think about the world treasure known as Sŏkkuram, I feel troubled. I still have doubts as to whether the restoration should have been done, and I also feel that I should do something about these problems.

The assumption that there was definitely a wooden antechamber is a modern idea. In terms of Shilla times, I think this is problematic.

As scholars, I feel that we should have strong convictions. In this sense, I respect Hwang Suyŏng. However, ...Sŏkkuram does not presently belong to one individual. The grotto must be Sŏkkuram, not the 'Hwang Kuram' In the end, it must belong to the world.

In conclusion, I'd like to suggest that all the people currently associated with the Sŏkkuram project be removed. Since there are many excellent young scholars in Korea, let some new people form a committee and take a fresh look at the grotto. If those previously associated with the grotto interfere, then we must wait until they all pass away. Then we can start afresh, assess possibilities and take things in a new direction. If we continue as we are now, there is so much bickering that nothing will ever get done.

I could finish my account of the Sŏkpulsa Temple grotto at this point, but it would be tragic and cruel to finish this story of glory and shame without leaving a glimmer of hope. I therefore intend to introduce two people who devoted their lives to the grotto, along with two poems.

KIM HYOGYŎNG'S TELEGRAPH

In 1966, Dr. Kim Hyogyŏng from Seoul National University's Engineering Department solved the grotto's moisture and moss problem (albeit by artificial means). I have never had the opportunity to meet Doctor Kim. Perhaps he is right in insisting that the dehumidifier could not be installed further away from the grotto; yet I am sure that the device will damage the cave in the long run.

In spite of these differences in opinion, Doctor Kim's sense of commitment has deeply impressed me. It made me feel that, as long as there are people like him, Korea is alive and has hope for the future.

On June 25, 1966, Kim Hyogyŏng installed a device to solve the grotto's moisture problem. At this point, he had fulfilled his responsibilities related to the grotto's preservation. Yet for the last 30 years, he has continued to oversee the dehumidifier project. No one has told him to do this, and he has not received a single penny from the Office of Cultural Properties or other organizations associated with Sŏkkuram. Although Doctor Kim has now retired from his position as professor, he continues to make trips to the grotto.

Since the dehumidifying unit was installed, the grotto's temperature and humidity have been checked five times a day at six and ten a.m., and two, six and ten p.m. The results are sent to Kyŏngju City and the Research Center of Cultural Properties. Doctor Kim also receives daily results to examine. Doctor Kim, now 81 years old, has been doing this since he was 48. In the "Sŏkkuram Specialists Conference Minutes", we find the following words from Doctor Kim:

According to the results thus far, the period from May to September presents the biggest problem. I therefore call to check with the machinery office every April...I don't recall when I was dismissed from my job as technical supervisor, but I make sure to go to the grotto several times a year. This is because around April and May, or August and September, I always get this urgent feeling calling me to the grotto. So I go to the site and give advice, showing the person in charge how to operate and manage the equipment, how to change the airfilters, etc. I feel it's best if the same person looks after things, and my visits help keep people on their toes.

I may sometimes be acting beyond my authority. Someone might complain why this Kim fellow keeps showing up with phoning first or without contacting the Office of Cultural Properties. Even so, I feel that since I installed this equipment in 1966, I should personally do this for as long as I am capable.

I cannot say that I have done my job well. Yet I am sure that the continuous data collected from the beginning up to now will serve as a basis for finding a better way to preserve the grotto.

While people tend to focus on the deeds of government officials, I have always believed that a culture flourishes when the average person does outstanding work. In our time, people want to do work that puts them in the limelight. We need people who stand firm as a rock regardless of what others say, stubbornly devoting their lives to a given task. Even if the 40 million inhabitants of Korea were to become unreliable half-wits who spend all their time dancing the reggae, Korean culture will never die as long as there are people like Doctor Kim. This is the lesson that the last century of Korean history has taught me.

At the Specialists' Conference, Doctor Kim talked about a personal incident that occurred when he was installing the equipment.

On June 25, 1966, I started up the dehumidifier, which completely removed all moisture from the air. When I went to bed, I lay awake until midnight, unable to get to sleep. Due to nagging concerns, I would visit the site a number of times in the year that followed. At this time, my children asked me where I was going all the time. I promised to tell them later, and then went down to Kyŏngju on June 26 and sent a telegram. I wrote, "Congratulations for having solved the moisture problem". In the 'From' column, I wrote, "the citizens of Kyŏngju". When I came home after work, my children told me that I had a telegram from the citizens of Kyŏngju. I told my wife, but not the children, that I had actually sent the message.

SŎK UIL, DIRECTOR OF THE SHILLA HISTORY AND SCIENCE MUSEUM

At 201 Ha-dong, deep within the Kyŏngju Folk and Handicrafts Village, one finds the Shilla History and Science Museum (Phone: 0561-745-4998). When it was first opened five years ago, the museum was known as the Tong'ak Art Gallery.

This museum, the greatest educational facility in all of Kyŏngju, was built through the sweat and determination of a Kyŏngju citizen. Those who attended the Sŏkkuram Specialists Conference in 1991 were deeply impressed by it. In fact, the general conclusion of the conference was that such facilities were needed throughout Korea.

The museum was originally built solely by Sŏk Uil (60 years old), the president of Seoul Kongyesa. President Sŏk went to Kyŏngju middle and high school, and then attended Sungkyunkwan University in Seoul where he majored in Oriental philosophy. After graduation, he devoted himself to selling building stone and stone carvings. He has no other qualification. Or, if he does, it would be that he has loved Kyŏngju more than anyone, has admired the ancient wisdom of Shilla and has aspired to take this great legacy from the past and present it within a modern, living educational facility.

In 1985, President Sŏk took the money he had earned through his business and began investing it in the museum. In order to help explain the great mysteries of the Sŏkpulsa Temple grotto, full and dissected models of Sŏkkuram were subsequently assembled. Other items in the museum's collection include an astronomical chart (based on Shilla astronomical knowledge as ascertained through research on Chŏmsŏngdae) and a "Diagram of the Royal Capital" (a map of Sŏrabŏl, i.e., ancient Kyŏngju, when it boasted 180,000 households). At present, the museum is working on a diagram showing the manufacturing process used to make the Emille Bell. In this way, the museum uses models, diagrams and photographs to teach visitors about ancient science.

The Sŏkkuram mock-ups include a 1/5-scale model and seven 1/10-scale models showing different aspects of the grotto's inside and outside. They also show the grotto's present form as well as a hypothetical model of the original. These models even deal with issues of academic debate such as the development of the antechamber, the arrangement of the guardian figures and the existence of a window in the dome. The grotto's science and precision, which inevitably have been discussed in an abstruse fashion in this book, are explained in full by these models. For this reason, anyone wanting to understand the mystery of Sŏkkuram should definitely visit this museum either before or after seeing the grotto.

This educational facility for Sǒkkuram was created not by the government, but privately. Sǒkkuram, on the other hand, collects extensive revenues from both Koreans and foreign travelers; yet the efforts of its administrators and the Office of Cultural Properties have amounted to nothing more than a glass window blocking access to the Buddha.

An Offering of Two Poems

Strangely enough, few poems have been written about the Sǒkpul Temple grotto. Poets can find all sorts of love and significance when looking at a rather mediocre creek; yet, when before the sacred Sǒkkuram Buddha, their praise has taken the form of silence.

I only know of four poems about Sǒkpul Temple. Of these, Yu Ch'ihwan's "Sǒkkuram Taebul" (Grand Buddha at Sǒkkuram) and Sǒ Chǒngju's "Sǒkkuram Kwanseǔmǔi Norae" (Song of Sǒkkuram's Avalokitesvara) are already well-known. Yu and Sǒ are two of Korea's most prominent poets, and they both loved Kyǒngju. Due to their personal attachment to the area, they evidently felt up to the task of writing about Sǒkkuram.

Yu Ch'ihwan (1908-1967, styled Chǒngma) spent ten years as principal of Kyǒngju High School and Kyǒngju Girls' High School. He moved away, but in his later years, wanted to return. Unfortunately, he died in a fatal accident before he had the chance to move back. His poetry includes the following piece about the Sǒkkuram Buddha.

> Resisting the urge to wail and keen,
> I have sat here as stone, with eyes shut,
> Yet notice beneath this thousand-year-old, cold skin,
> A vague coursing of blood, flowing of breath.
>
> ...

I feel

Wind through distant pines,

Blossoming lotuses on the East Sea,

Carefree cries of black magpies,

And the white moon setting insignificantly upon my forehead.

Who could understand!

But still resisting the urge to wail,

I sit as stone, quietly,

With eyes shut, legs crossed.

Yu Ch'ihwan's poetry has a fine, resonant quality and lacks complexity. When I memorized his famous poem "Kitpal" (Flag) in high school, I felt exhilarated as if I were standing on the ridge of a mountain. On the college entrance exam, I was fortunately given the question, "Fill in the blank with the first line of 'Kitpal'" (The answer: "This is a soundless outcry). Perhaps it was the excitement of seeing a familiar question or the misapplication of my own image-based memory techniques, but I answered, "This is a resounding outcry." Since I managed to squeeze by with a passing score, the test examiners evidently marked it correct.

At any rate, Yu Ch'ihwan's bold and cheerful poetry brings a tremendous sense of relief when one is troubled. However, his poems often fall apart after the strong first line. Perhaps this explains why the stele on the path from Pulguksa Temple to Sŏkkuram only contains the first two lines of Yu's poem.

The poetry of Sŏ Chŏngju (styled Midang, born 1915) always leaves a strong impression. Through quiet observation, he attains a subtle understanding of the living force behind phenomena. In this sense, he has attained the stage of complete understanding usually mentioned in Zen. However, even this calm poet could not write about Sŏkkuram without using an exclamation mark.

<blockquote>

With longing, I stand here,
A longing like a lake.

...

Oh! If only, if only such a person would appear,
One who loves 'me' more than I love myself,
One who loves a thousand years, a thousand years,
Would appear in the sunlight,

...

But I stand here.

...

Within this cool rock,
Day after day breathing in and out,
This blue breath,
Ah, it is still mine.

</blockquote>

HE WHO STRIKES THE BELL SHOULD...

Every year since 1980, I have gone up to the Sokpulsa Temple Grotto. Each time, I have found a way to spend several hours alone inside Sokkuram.

However, I didn't much care for the grotto during my visits in the 1980s. I preferred the collective peculiarity of the rather unpeculiar stone Buddhas at Unjusa Temple in Hwasun or the eccentric beauty dancing around the mouths of *changsŭng* (guardian posts) in villages near Mt.

THE FACE OF THE MAIN BUDDHA FIGURE *As a harmonious synthesis of the human and divine, the Buddha statue simultaneously expresses the ideal of humanity and the human manifestation of the divine.*

BODHISATTVA IN THE LEISURE POSTURE
Of the ten niche figures, this lovely Bodhisattva sitting in the
Leisure Posture impressed me the most.

Chirisan. Compared with these carvings, the Sŏkkuram Buddha seemed excessively authoritative, forceful and universal.

Then in the late 1980s, as I turned 40, I noticed something that previously had escaped my attention. Although I had been visiting for ten years, I saw for the first time the grotto's beautiful harmony.

On that day, I sensed something beyond the blind generalities of academia. The Buddha was too human to be called a god, yet with the dignity of an absolute power, it could neither be called human. It was too gentle to be stern, yet too austere to be compassionate. With its stately air, one could not say it looked young; yet it seemed too limber to be old. With bulging curves, it did not look masculine; yet it was too robust to be feminine. Along this line, someone once said, "It's too compassionate to be seen as a father; yet too strict to be seen as a mother." Indeed, this single carving seemed to embody all of this world's order and tranquillity.

While the main Buddha has a classical air, the Ten Disciples possess a vivid realism. Carved in bas-relief, the well-proportioned, slender figures of Manjusri, Samantabhadra, Indra and Brahma assume fanciful, idealized poses. The Eleven-Headed Avalokitesvara Bodhisattva, beautiful enough to have been 'Miss Unified Shilla', looks poised to walk out of the stone. Looking around the chamber, one sees Ksitigarbha Bodhisattva in a dignified pose and the layman Vimalakirti giving an eloquent talk. In one of the niches, another pretty Bodhisattva figure sits in the Leisure Posture with her body twisted and her chin resting on her hand as if nodding off. I have stood entranced for long periods, staring at these elegant figures.

Beauty is beauty. What more can I say? I can repeat the standard, hidebound description of the grotto as a great masterpiece combining religion, art and science, but beyond that I am speechless.

At this point, I concluded that, "Those who haven't laid eyes upon it, cannot talk about it since they haven't seen it. Those who have laid eyes upon it, cannot talk about it since they *have* seen it." Although I had deliberately rejected idealism and classicism, I was now captivated by these very movements. I could not deny the impact of this pure, aesthetic experience. After this, I felt the need to get to the heart of classical art so as to understand its profound aesthetic principles. But how was I to go about it? At that time, I recalled an aphorism I had once heard. It was a line from Ko Yusŏp's "What Can We Learn From Ancient Art?"[7]

The bell rings im proportion to the strength of the person hitting it...

1. The above is a back-translation of the Korean translation.
2. *Sŏkkuram suri kongsa pogosŏ.*
3. *Sŏkpulsa* (Seoul: Ilchogak 1990).
4. From the article "Sŏkkuram wonhyŏng pojonŭi wigi", *Shindong'a*, May 1969.
5. "Sŏkkuram wonhyŏng pojonŭi wigi".
6. "Sŏkkuram posunŭn kaeagi anida".
7. "Urinŭn kodae misulesŏ muŏsŭl paeul kŏsin'ga".

Note

In my former life, I must have been Korean, for there is no other way to explain the special affinity I feel for its land and people. Its mist-covered mountains covered with twisted pines and ancient temples have always had a special place in my heart. And yet there are probably few places so different from the American Northwest where I grew up. After all, the Northwest is characterized by large, empty spaces and an ancient history that has been largely annihilated and forgotten. Korea, on the other hand, is one of the most populated areas on earth, peopled not only by the living but also by the spirits of the dead. So in this sense, Korea's past is always superimposed upon its present. The country's ubiquitous relics and monuments are vivid reminders of past glories and uncounted sorrows. At the same time, they help us look beyond the recent past, during which Korea has been a powerless pawn in the power-struggles of the 20th century, to a time when it was one of the great civilizations of North-east Asia. These cultural artifacts also testify to Korea's tremendous vitality and perseverance, and suggest that, as Koreans reconnect with the vital roots of their culture, their nation will re-emerge as a leading cultural force.

Needless to say, I was greatly honored when asked to do this translation. Years before when I first came across Prof. Yu's books, I was immediately impressed by his insights, lovely writing style, sharp wit and detailed knowledge. In this respect, his work is somewhat unique among the books typically chosen for translation. Whereas many works on Korean cultural sites are little more than guide books, Prof. Yu's work provides the reader with a deeper perspective, explaining each site's significance instead of merely listing unrelated facts.

In cultural works, a number of dilemmas await the translator. Many terms have never been translated and have no Western equivalent. Other terms assume a knowledge of Korean culture and philosophy. The translator must always strike a balance between a literal translation that is accurate but incomprehensible and an interpretive translation that strays away from the author's original intent. While I have striven for the golden mean, I have undoubtedly fallen short at times. Thus all the awkward phrases and convoluted sentences found within this work must be attributed to the translator—they certainly do not exist in the original.

December 1999
Charles M. Mueller
the translator

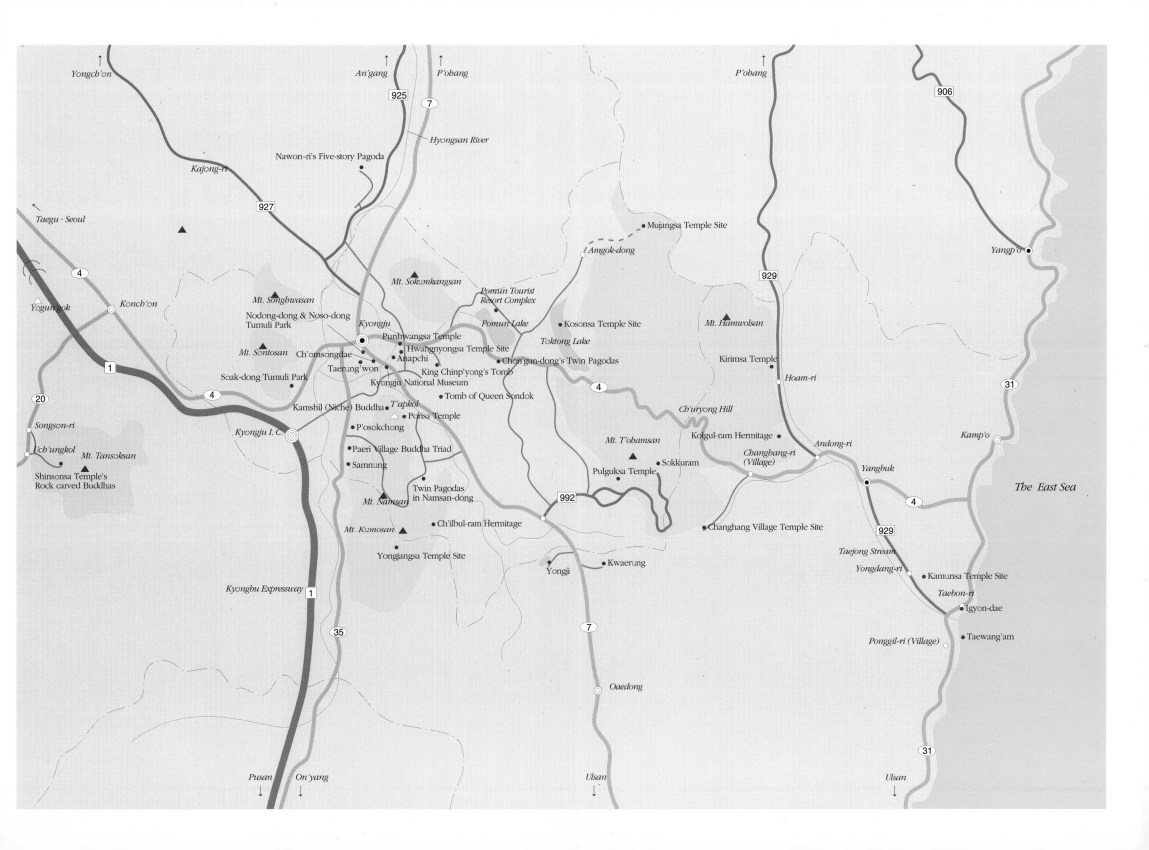